James Dabney McCabe

The Centennial History of the United States

James Dabney McCabe

The Centennial History of the United States

ISBN/EAN: 9783337404635

Printed in Europe, USA, Canada, Australia, Japan

Cover: Foto ©ninafisch / pixelio.de

More available books at **www.hansebooks.com**

THE
CENTENNIAL HISTORY

OF THE

UNITED STATES.

FROM

THE DISCOVERY

OF THE

AMERICAN CONTINENT

TO THE

CLOSE OF THE FIRST CENTURY

OF

AMERICAN INDEPENDENCE.

BY

JAMES D. McCABE,

AUTHOR OF "A MANUAL OF GENERAL HISTORY," "PATHWAYS OF THE HOLY LAND," "HISTORY OF THE WAR BETWEEN GERMANY AND FRANCE," "THE GREAT REPUBLIC," ETC., ETC.

EMBELLISHED WITH 442 FINE HISTORICAL ENGRAVINGS AND PORTRAITS.

Issued by subscription only, and not for sale in the book stores. Residents of any State desiring a copy should address the Publishers, and an Agent will call upon them. See page 927.

PUBLISHED BY

THE NATIONAL PUBLISHING COMPANY.

PHILADELPHIA, PA., CHICAGO, ILL., ST. LOUIS, MO., AND COLUMBUS, OHIO.

CHAPTER XLI.

THE ADMINISTRATION OF ABRAHAM LINCOLN—THE CIVIL WAR.

Inauguration of President Lincoln—His History—The Confederate Commissioners at Washington—Attack upon Fort Sumter by the Confederates—The President calls for Troops—Response of the North and West—Secession of the Border States—Opening Events of the War in Virginia—Withdrawal of West Virginia—Admitted into the Union as a separate State—Meeting of Congress—The West Virginia Campaign—Battle of Bull Run—The War in Missouri—Kentucky Occupied—The Blockade—Capture of Port Royal—The "Trent" Affair—Insurrection in East Tennessee—State of Affairs at the Opening of the Year 1862—Edwin M. Stanton made Secretary of War—Capture of Forts Henry and Donelson—The Confederates fall back from Kentucky—Battle of Shiloh—Capture of Island No. 10—Evacuation of Corinth—Capture of Memphis—Bragg's Kentucky Campaign—His Retreat into Tennessee—Battles of Iuka and Corinth—Battle of Murfreesboro', or Stone River—Grant's Campaign against Vicksburg—Its Failure—The War beyond the Mississippi—Battle of Pea Ridge—Capture of Roanoke Island—Capture of New Orleans—Surrender of Fort Pulaski—The War in Virginia—Johnston's Retreat from Centreville—Battle between the "Monitor" and "Virginia"—The Move to the Peninsula—Johnston Retreats to the Chickahominy—Battle of Seven Pines—Jackson's Successes in the Valley of Virginia—The Seven Days' Battles before Richmond—Battle of Cedar Mountain—Defeat of General Pope's Army—Lee Invades Maryland—Capture of Harper's Ferry—Battles of South Mountain and Antietam—Retreat of Lee into Virginia—McClellan Removed—Battle of Fredericksburg.

ABRAHAM LINCOLN, the sixteenth president of the United States, was inaugurated at Washington on the 4th of March, 1861. As it was feared that an attempt would be made to prevent the inauguration, the city was held by a strong body of regular troops, under General Scott, and the president-elect was escorted from his hotel to the capitol by a military force. No effort was made to interfere with the ceremonies, and the inauguration passed off quietly.

The new president was in his fifty-third year, and was a native of Kentucky. When he was but eight years old his father removed to Indiana, and the boyhood of the future president was spent in hard labor upon the farm. Until he reached manhood he continued to lead this life, and during this entire period attended school for only a year. At the age of twenty-one he removed to Illinois, where he began life as a storekeeper. Being anxious to rise above his humble position, he determined to study law. He was too poor to buy the necessary books, and so borrowed them from a neighboring lawyer, read them at night, and returned them in the morning. His genial character, great good nature, and love of humor, won him the friendship of the people among whom he resided, and they elected him to the lower house of the legislature of Illinois. He now abandoned his mercantile pursuits, and began the practice of the law, and was subsequently elected a representative to Congress from the Springfield district. He took an active part in the politics of his State, and in 1858 was the candidate of the Republican party for United States senator. In this capacity he engaged in a series of debates in various parts of the State with Senator Douglas, the Democratic candidate for re-election to the same position. This debate was remarkable for its brilliancy and intellectual vigor, and brought him prominently before the whole country, and opened the way to his nomination for the presidency. In person he was tall and ungainly, and in manner he was rough and awkward, little versed in the refinements of society. He was a man, however, of great natural vigor of intellect, and was possessed of a fund of strong common sense, which enabled him to see at a glance through the shams by which he was surrounded, and to pursue his own aims with singleness of heart and directness of purpose. He had sprung from the ranks of the people, and he was never false to them. He was a simple, unaffected, kind-hearted man; anxious to do his duty to the whole country; domestic in his tastes and habits; and incorruptible in every relation of life. He was fond of humor, and overflowed with it; finding in his "little stories" the only relaxation he ever sought from the heavy cares of the trying position upon which he was now entering. He selected his cabinet from the leading men of the Republican party, and placed William H. Seward, of New York, at its head as secretary of state.

ABRAHAM LINCOLN.

Mr. Lincoln was sincerely anxious to avoid everything which might precipitate the civil strife; but at the same time was determined to maintain the authority of the general government over the seceded States. In his inaugural address he declared his purpose to collect the public revenues at the ports of the seceded States, and to "hold, occupy, and possess" the forts, arsenals, and other public property seized by those States. At the time of his entrance upon the duties of his office Fort Sumter and Fort Pickens were still held by the federal forces.

The Confederate government was convinced that war was inevitable;

and since its inauguration had been preparing for the coming struggle. Nearly all the officers of the army and navy of the United States, who were natives of the seceded States, resigned their commissions in the old service, and were given similar positions in the army of the Confederate States. The forces collected at Charleston and Pensacola were reinforced

ARRIVAL OF PRESIDENT LINCOLN AT THE CAPITOL.

by troops from other States, and the command at the former place was conferred upon General Pierre G. T. Beauregard, and at the latter upon General Braxton Bragg, both of whom had been distinguished officers of the old army.

Just before the close of Mr. Buchanan's term of office the Confederate government despatched John Forsyth, of Alabama, Martin J. Crawford, of Georgia, and A. B. Roman, of Louisiana, to Washington as commissioners to endeavor to effect a peaceable adjustment of the matters at issue between the two governments, and to treat for an equitable division of the public property of the United States. Mr. Buchanan refused to receive the commissioners in their official capacity, and after the inauguration of the new administration they addressed a note to Mr. Seward, the new secretary of state, setting forth the objects of their mission, and soliciting an official interview with the president. Mr. Seward declined to receive them in their official capacity, but answered them verbally through Mr. Justice John A. Campbell, of the Supreme Court of the United States, that he was in favor of a peaceful settlement of the difficulty, and that the troops would be withdrawn from Fort Sumter in less than ten days. Mr. Seward's object appears to have been to deceive the

STATE-HOUSE, SPRINGFIELD, ILLINOIS.

commissioners, and lull their suspicions, in order to gain time for the preparations which had been determined upon for the relief of Fort Sumter.

In the meantime, the government having resolved to reinforce and provision Fort Sumter at all hazards, every nerve was strained to carry out this design before it should become known to the Confederates. An expedition consisting of seven ships, carrying two hundred and eighty-five guns and twenty-four hundred men, was prepared at New York and Norfolk. The southern commissioners, whose suspicions had been allayed by Mr. Seward's message, were alarmed by the rumors of these preparations, which they suspected were for the relief of Fort Sumter. They waited upon Judge Campbell to ask an explanation, and that gentleman, on the 7th of April, addressed a note to Mr. Seward asking if the assurances he had given were well or ill founded. Mr. Seward replied as follows: " Faith as to Sumter fully kept; wait and see."

In the meantime the expedition had sailed from New York and Norfolk, and was on its way to Charleston harbor. On the 8th of April, 1861, Governor Pickens, of South Carolina, was notified by the general government of its intention to relieve Fort Sumter at all hazards, and of the sailing of the fleet for that purpose. Governor Pickens at once informed General Beauregard of this notification, and the news was telegraphed by him to the Confederate government at Montgomery.

The Confederate secretary of war thereupon ordered General Beauregard to demand the immediate surrender of Fort Sumter; "and if this should be refused to proceed to reduce it." On the 11th of April General Beauregard demanded of Major Anderson the surrender of the fort.

FORT SUMTER.

The demand was refused in writing; but Major Anderson added verbally to the messenger, " I will await the first shot, and if you do not batter us to pieces, we will be starved out in a few days." Beauregard telegraphed this remark with Anderson's reply to his government, and was answered, " Do not desire needlessly to bombard Fort Sumter. If Major Anderson will state the time at which, as indicated by himself, he will evacuate, and agree that, in the meantime, he will not use his guns against us unless ours should be employed against Fort Sumter, you are authorized thus to avoid the effusion of blood. If this or its equivalent be refused, reduce the fort, as your judgment decides most practicable." The federal fleet was on its way to Charleston, and if the attack of the Confederates was to be made at all, no time was to be lost. General Beauregard, therefore, gave Major Anderson warning that he should open fire upon Fort Sumter at half-past four o'clock the next morning.

At the designated hour on the morning of April 12th, the Confederate batteries opened fire upon Fort Sumter, which replied to them with spirit. The bombardment lasted over thirty-two hours, and the fort was greatly damaged, and many of the guns were dismounted. The fleet arrived off the harbor during the bombardment, but remained in the offing, and took no part in the engagement. Not a single life was lost in this memorable battle. Late in the afternoon of the 13th, Major Anderson agreed to capitulate, and the firing ceased. The victors granted liberal terms to Anderson and his men, whose heroism had aroused their warmest admiration; and on the morning of Sunday, April 14th, the fort was surrendered to the Confederate forces, and Major Anderson and the garrison embarked in one of the vessels of the fleet, which at once sailed for New York.

The attack upon Fort Sumter put an end to the last hope of peace, and aroused the most intense excitement in both sections of the country. On the 15th of April President Lincoln issued a proclamation calling upon the States to furnish seventy-five thousand troops for the suppression of the rebellion, and convening Congress in extra session on the 4th of July. The Northern and Western States responded with enthusiasm to the president's call for troops, and at once began to forward their quotas to the points designated by the war department.

The enthusiasm in the south was fully equal to that of the north. The Confederate government issued a call for volunteers to repel the threatened invasion of the federal forces, and it was responded to with alacrity.

Until now the States of Maryland, Virginia, North Carolina, Tennessee, Kentucky, Arkansas and Missouri, generally known as the Border States, had remained in the Union, hoping to be able to effect a peaceable settlement of the quarrel. Their sympathies were with the Southern States, and it was generally believed that in the event of war they would cast their lots with those States. Each of these States was included in the call of President Lincoln for troops. The governors of most of them replied by refusing to furnish the quotas required of them, and by denouncing the president's demand as illegal. Conventions of the people were held, and all but Maryland, Kentucky and Missouri withdrew from the Union. The secession of Virginia took place on the 17th of April; that of Arkansas on the 6th of May; that of North Carolina on the 20th of May; and that of Tennessee on the 8th of June. These States subsequently ratified the constitution of the Confederate States, and became members of the new republic. Kentucky and Missouri remained neutral.

The passage of the act of secession by the Virginia convention was kept secret for a day or two in order to give the authorities of that State an opportunity to seize the United States arsenal at Harper's Ferry, and the navy yard at Portsmouth. The officer in command of the arsenal, upon hearing of the approach of a force of Virginia troops, destroyed a number of the muskets stored there, set fire to the buildings, and re-treated into Pennsylvania. The Virginians extinguished the flames and secured a large quantity of arms and equipments and the valuable ma-chinery for the manufacture of arms. The commandant of the navy yard at Portsmouth, upon the approach of the Virginians, made no attempt to defend his post, but spiked the cannon, burned or sunk the war vessels lying in the harbor, set fire to the buildings, and retreated with two war

HARPER'S FERRY.

steamers. The navy yard was at once occupied by the Virginians, who secured nearly two thousand pieces of cannon, and an immense quantity of stores and munitions of all kinds. The governors of the seceded Border States issued calls for volunteers immediately upon the withdrawal of their States. Men came forward in such large numbers that arms could not be provided for all of them. The prominent points of danger in Virginia were occupied and fortified by the State troops; but the con-trol of the military affairs in all the Border States soon passed into the hands of the Confederate government.

As it was certain that the first operations of the war would take place upon the borders of Virginia, the city of Richmond was made the capital

50

of the Confederate States, and on the 21st of May the Confederate government was removed to that city.

The western part of the State of Virginia refused to join the remainder of the State in its withdrawal from the Union. On the 11th of June, 1861, the people of the western counties met in convention at Wheeling, declared their independence of the old State, organized a State government, and proclaimed their intention to remain faithful to the Union. The action of this convention was sustained by the federal government, and on the 26th of November, 1861, another convention met at Wheeling, and adopted a constitution for the new State of West Virginia. This constitution was ratified by the people at the polls on the 3d of May, 1862, and application was made for the admission of West Virginia into the Union as a State, which was accomplished by act of Congress on the 20th of June, 1863.

In the meantime the federal government set to work with energy to prepare for the struggle before it. The call of President Lincoln for troops had been answered by three hundred thousand volunteers. On

COAT OF ARMS OF WEST VIRGINIA.

the 17th of April, two days after the president's proclamation, the Sixth Massachusetts regiment left Boston for Washington. In passing through Baltimore it was attacked by a crowd of citizens who sympathized with the south, and three soldiers were killed and eight wounded. Several citizens were killed and wounded. The regiment reached Washington the same day, and was soon joined by other troops from the Northern States. In a short time the force at the capital was sufficient to put an end to all fears for its safety. Alexandria and the Virginia shore opposite Washington were seized and fortified. Baltimore was occupied by a force under General Butler, and the communications of Washington with the north and west were made sure. On the 19th of April the president issued a proclamation declaring all the southern ports in a state of blockade ; and on the 3d of May he put forth another proclamation ordering the regular army of the United States to be increased to sixty-four thousand seven hundred and forty-eight men, and the navy to eighteen thousand seamen. On the 10th of May he issued a fourth proclamation, suspending the writ of *habeas corpus* in certain localities, and authority to suspend this privilege was conferred upon the commanders of military departments soon afterward.

Under the instructions of the government these commanders now proceeded to arrest great numbers of persons in various parts of the country who were suspected of sympathizing with the south. They were imprisoned at the military posts, and were denied trial by the civil courts. John Merryman, a citizen of Maryland, was one of the persons so arrested. His friends applied for redress to the chief-justice of the United States, who held the suspension of the *habeas corpus* act by the president to be unconstitutional, and ordered the discharge of the prisoner. The government paid no attention to this decision, and held the prisoner in confinement. A little later the legislature of Maryland, which was strongly southern in its sympathies, was prevented from meeting by the sudden arrest and imprisonment of a large number of its members by order of the secretary of war.

On the 4th of July, 1861, Congress convened in extra session at Washington, in accordance with the president's proclamation. This body proceeded to give to the government a prompt and effectual support. Resolutions were introduced to legalize the extraordinary acts of the president in setting aside the writ of *habeas corpus*, in ordering the arbitrary arrest and confinement of citizens, and in assuming certain other powers which belonged to Congress. Congress refused to throw over these acts, however necessary, the sanction of the law; but in view of the necessity of prompt and vigorous action on the part of the president excused his acts on the distinct ground of the "necessities of war." Measures were adopted without delay for putting in the field an army of five hundred and twenty-five thousand men, and for equipping a powerful navy; and the sum of five hundred millions of dollars was appropriated for the prosecution of the war. During this session Congress also adopted a solemn resolution declaring " that this war is not prosecuted on our part in any spirit of oppression, nor for any purpose of conquest or subjugation, nor for the purpose of overthrowing or interfering with the rights or established institutions of those [the seceded] States; but to defend and maintain the supremacy of the constitution and all laws made in pursuance thereof, and to preserve the Union with all the dignity, equality and rights of the several States unimpaired; that as soon as these objects are accomplished the war ought to cease."

In the meantime the Confederates had collected troops at important points to resist the advance of the federal troops into Virginia. A force under Brigadier-General Garnett was stationed in West Virginia to cover the approaches from that direction; Harper's Ferry, which commanded the entrance into the valley of Virginia, was held by an army of seven thousand or eight thousand men, under General Joseph E. Johnston; a much larger force, under General Beauregard, took position near Manassas Junction, about thirty miles from Washington; and a column of several thousand men, under General John B. Magruder, was stationed at York-town, on the peninsula between the York and James rivers, to cover Richmond from the direction of Fortress Monroe at the mouth of Hampton Roads, which was still held by the federal troops. Norfolk was also held by a strong force. With the exception of that occupied by General Garnett's command, all these positions were carefully fortified.

The Union army at Fortress Monroe numbered about twelve thousand men, and was commanded by General B. F. Butler. Early in June, Magruder moved a force of eighteen hundred men and several pieces of artillery from Yorktown, and took position at Bethel Church, about half

STATE HOUSE, COLUMBUS, OHIO.

way between Yorktown and Hampton. On the 10th of June he was attacked by a force of four thousand troops under General Pierce, of Massachusetts, but succeeded in repulsing the attack and maintaining his position.

In the opposite quarter of the State, the Union forces were more successful. In order to prevent the Confederates from overrunning West Virginia, a strong body of Ohio and Indiana troops under General George B. McClellan was sent into that region. McClellan set to work at once to drive the Confederates out of West Virginia, and on the 3d of June a portion of his command under General Kelley defeated General

Garnett at Philippi. McClellan now advanced against the main body of Garnett's forces. On the 11th of July he attacked the command of Colonel Pegram at Rich Mountain, and defeated it. This defeat compelled General Garnett to fall back towards the valley of Virginia. He was pursued by McClellan and overtaken at Carrick's ford, on the Cheat river. In the battle which ensued here Garnett was killed, and the remnant of his command was driven beyond the mountains.

The United States had assembled a considerable army of volunteers and regulars at Washington under Major-General Irwin McDowell. On the 24th of May Alexandria, on the Virginia side of the Potomac, nine miles below Washington, was seized by a detachment from this army. Its commander, Colonel Ellsworth, was killed by a citizen. Strong defences were erected on the Virginia shore between Washington and Alexandria, and the army was encamped within these lines. Two months were passed in organizing and disciplining this force, and in the meantime the people of the Northern and Western States became impatient of the delay, and demanded an immediate advance upon the southern army and Richmond.

Preparatory to his own advance General McDowell sent General Patterson with twenty thousand men to cross the Potomac at Williamsport, and prevent General Johnston from leaving the valley and joining Beauregard at Manassas. Upon the arrival of Patterson on the upper Potomac, General Johnston evacuated Harper's Ferry and took position at Winchester. Patterson made a considerable show of force in the valley, but refrained from attacking Johnston, although the latter sought to induce him to do so. He took position about nine miles from Winchester, and remained inactive there.

In the meantime the preparations for the advance of McDowell's army were completed, and on the 17th of July he began his march from the Potomac towards Bull Run, on the banks of which the Confederates were posted. His army numbered over fifty thousand men, and forty-nine pieces of artillery. As soon as the advance of this army was known to him, General Beauregard informed General Johnston of it, and begged him to come to his assistance. Johnston skilfully eluded Patterson's army, and hastened to Bull Run, arriving there with a part of his command in time to take part in the battle.

The Confederate army had taken position behind Bull Run, and in advance of Manassas Junction. Including the force brought by General Johnston, who assumed the chief command by virtue of his rank, it consisted of thirty-one thousand four hundred and thirty-one men and fifty-five guns.

On the 18th of July General McDowell attempted to force a passage of Bull Run at Blackburn's ford, but was repulsed. On the morning of the 21st, the Union army advanced in force, and endeavored to turn the left of the southern line. An obstinately-contested battle ensued, which lasted from sunrise until nearly sunset. It resulted in the total defeat of the federal army, which was driven back in utter rout upon Alexandria and Washington, with a loss of between four and five thousand men in killed, wounded and prisoners, and twenty-eight pieces of artillery.

For a while the effects of this disaster upon the federal army were so great that Washington was almost defenceless; but the Confederates made no effort to follow up their victory. They were almost as badly demoralized by their success as the Union army by its defeat.

Recovering from the dismay of its first great reverse, the government went to work with vigor to repair the disaster. The levy of five hundred thousand men ordered by Congress was raised promptly and without difficulty, so eager was the desire of the people to wipe out the disgrace of Bull Run. At his own request General Scott, whose bodily infirmities were so great as to render him unable to discharge the duties of his position, was relieved of the command of the army. Major-General George B. McClellan was given the chief command of the armies of the Union, and ordered to take charge of the force assembling before Washington, which was named the Army of the Potomac. He devoted himself with success to the task of organizing and disciplining the recruits which came pouring in during the fall and winter.

GEN. P. G. T. BEAUREGARD.

The remainder of the year 1861 passed away quietly on the Potomac, with the single exception of the battle of Leesburg. Colonel Baker with a force of two thousand men was sent by General Stone to cross the Potomac at Edward's ferry, and drive back the Confederate force under General Evans from its position near Leesburg. He made his attack on the 21st of October, but was repulsed with the loss of eight hundred killed and wounded, being himself among the slain. The Confederate army held its position at Centreville through the fall and winter, and at one time its outposts were pushed forward within view of the city of Washington.

In the fall of 1861 an army of ten thousand men was sent by the Confederate government into the valley of Virginia to prevent its occupation by the federal forces. The command of these troops was conferred upon

General T. J. Jackson, whose conspicuous gallantry at Bull Run had won him the sobriquet of "Stonewall Jackson," by which he was afterwards known by both armies. He established his head-quarters at Winchester.

In the meantime the war had been going on in western Virginia. After the transfer of General McClellan to Washington the command of the Union forces passed to Brigadier-General Rosecranz, an able officer. He had several indecisive encounters with the commands of Generals Floyd and Wise in the region of the Gauley and New rivers. General Robert E. Lee was sent by the Confederate government to assume the chief command in the west. He attacked the brigade of General Reynolds at Cheat mountain on the 14th of September, but was repulsed and obliged to retreat. On the 4th of October General Reynolds attacked a Confederate force under General Henry R. Jackson on the Greenbrier river, but was repulsed.

The State of Missouri took no part in the secession movements of the spring of 1861. Her people were divided; a large party sympathized with the south; but a still larger party was determined that the State should remain in the Union. These parties soon came in conflict. The governor and leading officials of the State were in favor of secession, and used all their influence to bring about the withdrawal of Missouri from the Union. A camp of the State militia was formed near St. Louis, and was called Camp Jackson in honor of the governor. It was known that the force assembled at this camp was intended to serve as a nucleus around which an army hostile to the federal government might assemble. By extraordinary exertions Colonel Francis P. Blair, Jr., a member of Congress from St. Louis, and Captain Nathaniel Lyon, commanding the troops at the Jefferson barracks, near St. Louis, succeeded in collecting a force of five regiments of Union volunteers. On the 10th of May, 1861, Lyon with these five regiments suddenly surrounded Camp Jackson, and compelled General Frost, the commanding officer, to surrender his whole force, camp and equipments. By this prompt action the State forces were prevented from carrying out their plan for seizing the United States arsenal at St. Louis, which contained sixty thousand stand of arms of the latest patterns, and a number of cannon, and a large quantity of ammunition. For this decisive action Captain Lyon was commissioned a brigadier-general by the president.

Satisfied that the desire of the southern party in Missouri to remain neutral was but a pretext to gain time to arm the State for a union with the Confederates, President Lincoln determined to compel all the State forces not in the federal service to disband. An interview was held at St. Louis on the 11th of June between Governor Jackson and General

ST LOUIS, 1875.

792

Lyon, now commanding the federal troops in Missouri. Governor Jackson demanded that no United States forces should be quartered in or marched through Missouri. General Lyon refused to comply with this demand, and insisted that the State forces should be disbanded, pledging himself to respect the rights and privileges of the State. At the close of the interview the governor returned to Jefferson City, the capital of the State, and the next day, the 12th, issued his proclamation calling fifty thousand of the State militia into active service for the purpose of driving the federal troops from the State, and protecting the "lives, liberty and property of the citizens." General Lyon at once marched upon Jefferson City, and occupied it on the 15th, the governor and his supporters having retired to the interior of the State. On the 17th Lyon proceeded to Booneville and defeated the State troops stationed there under General Price.

GEN. STERLING PRICE.

The southwestern part of Missouri is rich in deposits of lead, and valuable mines of this mineral are worked there. The State authorities were anxious to hold this region, as it was of the highest importance to them to obtain the use of these mines to supply their army with lead. A column of federal troops under General Sigel was sent by General Lyon to intercept the retreat of the State troops. On the 5th of July Sigel attacked the State troops under Governor Jackson at Carthage, but was repulsed.

The next day, July 6th, Governor Jackson was joined at Carthage by General Sterling Price, of the Missouri State Guard, and General Ben McCulloch, of the Confederate army, with several thousand men. The command of the whole force was conferred upon General McCulloch, who had been ordered by his government to advance into Missouri. The southern army,

MAJOR-GENERAL F. SIGEL.

according to General McCulloch's statement, numbered fifty-three hundred infantry, six thousand mounted men, and fifteen pieces of artillery. It advanced rapidly into the interior of the State, and on the 9th of August reached Wilson's creek, near Springfield. General Lyon had taken position there with a force somewhat smaller than that of the Confederates. On the morning of the 10th he attacked the southern army. The battle lasted six hours, and was hotly contested. General Lyon was killed at the head of his troops while endeavoring to turn the left flank of the Confederates, and his army was forced back.   His body was left in the hands of the Confederates, who treated it with becoming respect.

Springfield was occupied by the Confederates the day after the battle; but McCulloch and Price being unable to agree upon the plan of the campaign, they soon withdrew to the Arkansas border.   The Union army after the battle withdrew to Rolla, near the centre of the State.

A few weeks later General Price with a force of over five thousand Confederates laid siege to Lexington, on the Missouri river, which was held by about three thousand men under Colonel Mulligan.   After a gallant defence Mulligan was forced to surrender on the 20th of September.

Major-General John C. Fremont was now appointed by President Lincoln to take command of the western army.   He forced Price's command back into the southwestern part of the State.   Arriving near Springfield, Fremont prepared to bring the Confederates to a decisive engagement, but on the 2d of November was removed from his command.   He was succeeded by General Hunter, who abandoned the pursuit, and fell back to St. Louis.   On the 18th of November Hunter was superseded by Major-General Halleck, who by a rapid advance drove Price once more towards the Arkansas border.   This movement closed the campaign of 1861 in Missouri.   The Union army had not only saved the State to the Union, but had confined the Confederates to the Arkansas border.

MAJ.-GEN. N. LYON.

In the meantime Governor Jackson had summoned the legislature of Missouri to meet at Neosho.   It assembled at that place in October, passed an ordinance of secession, and elected delegates and senators to the Confederate Congress.   Though this action was merely formal, and received the support of but a small part of the people of Missouri, it was recognized as valid by the Confederate government, and Missouri was proclaimed one of the Confederate States.

The governor and State authorities of Kentucky attempted at the outset of the war to hold the position of armed neutrality between the parties to the contest; but as in the case of Missouri, this effort failed.   Neither the federal government nor that of the Southern Confederacy could, in the nature of things, respect this neutrality.   The federal troops were poured into Kentucky, and the Confederates seized Columbus, on the Mississippi, Bowling Green, in the centre of the State, and other positions in the western part.   The southern party in Kentucky, within the protection of the Confederate lines, organized a provisional government for the State, sent senators and representatives to the Congress at Richmond, which formally recognized Kentucky as one of the Confederate States.

The force at Columbus was commanded by General Polk of the Confederate army. At Belmont, on the Missouri shore of the river, immediately opposite Columbus, a body of Confederate troops was stationed. On the 7th of November, General U. S. Grant having descended the Mississippi from Cairo, attacked the force at Belmont with his command of three thousand men. After a sharp struggle he was repulsed, and forced to retreat to Cairo.

At the outset of the war the Confederates occupied the principal ports of the south, and a number of prominent points on the Atlantic coast.

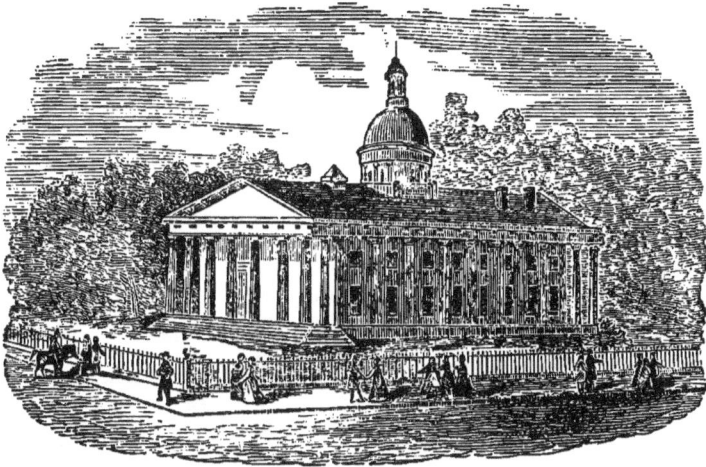

STATE HOUSE, INDIANAPOLIS, INDIANA.

These were fortified by them as well as the means at hand would permit. The general government resolved to capture these as rapidly as possible, as their reduction was necessary in order to render the blockade of the southern coast effectual. The first expedition was despatched from Fortress Monroe in August, 1861, under Commodore Stringham and General Butler, and was directed against the Confederate works at Hatteras inlet, which commanded the entrance to Albemarle and Pamlico sounds. These works were captured on the 29th of August.

The great extent of the coast to be blockaded by the navy made it necessary that a good harbor at some central point should be secured, where supplies could be stored for the fleet, and where vessels could refill without returning to the northern ports. Port Royal Harbor in South

Carolina was selected as the best place for this purpose. It was defended by Fort Walker on Hilton Head and Fort Beauregard on the opposite side of the harbor. A powerful naval and military expedition under Commodore Dupont and General Thomas W. Sherman attacked these works on the 7th of November, and reduced them after a terrible bombardment by the fleet. Port Royal was at once occupied by the expedition, and during the war was the principal depot on the southern coast for the fleets and armies of the Union.

LIEUTENANT-GENERAL POLK.

It was not possible, however, to render the blockade effective. Great efforts were made to increase the number of vessels employed in this duty, but the Confederates succeeded in eluding the Union cruisers almost at pleasure, and a steady communication was maintained between the southern ports and England by way of the West Indies. A number of armed vessels in the service of the confederacy succeeded in getting to sea. By the close of the year they had inflicted severe damage upon the commerce of the Northern States, and had almost driven the foreign trade of the United States from the ocean.

During the early part of the war the southern government was encouraged to hope that the governments of England and France would recognize the independence of the Confederate States, and in the fall of 1861, James M. Mason of Virginia and John Slidell of Louisiana were ordered to proceed to Europe, as commissioners from the Confederate States, to secure this recognition. They sailed from Charleston on the 12th of October, and reached Cuba in safety. There they took passage for England on board the British mail-steamer "Trent." Hearing of this, Captain Wilkes, of the United States war-steamer "San Jacinto," overhauled the "Trent" upon the high seas, boarded her, and seized the

JAMES M. MASON.

two commissioners and their secretaries and sailed with them to Boston harbor, where they were imprisoned in one of the forts.

The "Trent" in the meantime proceeded on her voyage, and upon reaching England her commander informed the British government of the outrage that had been committed upon its flag. The English government at once demanded of President Lincoln the immediate and unconditional release of the Confederate commissioners and satisfaction for the insult to its flag. It was understood that France was prepared to sustain England in her demands. The Federal government disavowed the action of Captain Wilkes in seizing the commissioners, and those gentlemen were released and allowed to continue their voyage. They reached England in due time. Mr. Mason proceeded to London and Mr. Slidell to France. Neither the English nor the French governments would receive the commissioners officially. It was understood that the United States would regard the interference of either in the American quarrel as a cause of war, and neither power cared to join in the struggle.

Tennessee seceded from the Union, as we have related, in the spring of 1861. The western and central portions of the State were unanimously in favor of joining the Southern States and gave a hearty support to the confederacy during the war, but East Tennessee, inhabited by a race of hardy mountaineers, was devoted to the Union, and was unwilling to leave it. In the autumn of 1861 the East Tennesseeans took up arms against the Confederate government, and began to destroy the railway bridges in that part of the State. This movement was full of danger to the confederacy, as the principal line of com- munication between Virginia and the Missis- sippi passed through East Tennessee. A con- siderable force of Confederate troops was sent into East Tennessee to hold the people in sub- jection and protect the railroads, but throughout

JOHN SLIDELL.

the war the hostility of the people of this region was a constant source of danger and of weakness to the Confederates.

When the year 1862 opened, the war had assumed colossal proportions. The military operations extended almost across the continent, and engaged a number of powerful armies, and a formidable navy. The call of Presi- dent Lincoln for troops had been cheerfully responded to, and the opening of the year found the United States provided with a force of over half a million of men, splendidly armed and equipped, and supplied with every- thing necessary for the successful prosecution of the war. The north had profited by its first reverses, and was resolved that its next effort, which was to be made at the opening of the season for active operations, should find it thoroughly prepared for the task it had undertaken. A cordial support was given to the measures of the government by the people. Its wants were supplied by means of a heavy loan which was readily negoti- ated with the capitalists of the Eastern States. From the moment that the despondency caused by the reverse at Bull Run had subsided sufficiently to enable the people of the loyal States to face the situation calmly, every one saw that the work of preparation must all be done over from the beginning, and it was done bravely and thoroughly. During the fall and winter the army was rapidly increased; vessels were purchased and built for the navy.

The southern armies, on the other hand, had grown steadily weaker. The first successes of the Confederate troops had greatly demoralized the southern people. Volunteering soon ceased almost entirely. Even the heaviest bounties failed to bring recruits. There was a widespread delusion throughout the south that the war was practically ended. The measures of the Confederate Congress steadily thinned, instead of filling up the ranks of the southern armies, and when the new year dawned there was grave reason to fear that the spring campaign would find the south without an adequate army unless more vigorous measures were resorted to. It was exceedingly doubtful whether the troops already in the service would renew their enlistments, which expired in the spring of 1862. During the winter the Southern Congress adopted a law granting a furlough and a heavy bounty to every soldier who would re-enlist for the war. The furlough was to be granted during the winter; the bounty to be paid at a later period. Many of those who went home on these furloughs did so with the intention of remaining there; and the practical effect of the measure was to diminish the strength of the Confederate armies. At length the Confederate Congress was driven by the necessities of the situation to adopt a most stringent and sweeping measure. On the 16th of April, 1862, a conscription act was passed, giving to the president of the confederacy the power to call into the military service the entire male population of the various States between the ages of eighteen and thirty-five years. In September, 1862, a second act was passed extending the conscript age to forty-five years. The measure was acquiesced in by the southern people, but was never popular with them. It served the purpose for which it was intended, however, and enabled the Confederate government to collect a force of several hundred thousand men in the spring of 1862, and thus to fill up the ranks of its armies in the field, and to retain the regiments already in the service.

When the spring opened, General Halleck, whose head-quarters were at St. Louis, held Missouri against the Confederates with a powerful army. General Buell, with a considerable force, was stationed in central Kentucky. In his front an inferior force of Confederates, under General Albert Sidney Johnston, held Bowling Green and covered Nashville and the Tennessee and Cumberland rivers. They also held Columbus and other prominent points on the Mississippi. The army of the Potomac, under General McClellan, lay along the Potomac, confronting the Confederate army of Northern Virginia, which held Centreville. A considerable force was collected at Fortress Monroe; and an army of about ten thousand Confederates, under Magruder, held a strongly fortified line extending from Yorktown across the peninsula to the James river. In addition to these forces, the Federal government had collected a powerful flotilla of steamers and gunboats at Cairo, the junction of the Ohio and Mississippi rivers, to assist in the operations of the western armies. The capture of New Orleans had been resolved upon, and a combined naval and military expedition under Commodore Farragut and General Butler was assembled for that purpose; and another expedition was organized in the Chesapeake for the reduction of Roanoke island and the forts on the North Carolina coast.

Soon after the opening of the new year, Mr. Cameron, whose administration of the war department had failed to give satisfaction to the country, was removed by President Lincoln, and sent to Russia as minister from the United States. The president on the 13th of January appointed Edwin M. Stanton, of Ohio, secretary of war. The new secretary was confessedly one of the ablest men in America, and his accession to the control of the war department infused new life into the military preparations of the government. During the remainder of the war he occupied this position, and it is not too much to say that his vigorous administration of his department was one of the chief causes of the final success of the Union arms.

Active operations were resumed earlier in the west than in the east. On the 19th of January General George H. Thomas drove the Confederates under General Zollicoffer from Mill Spring in Kentucky. The defeated force had held the right of the Confederate line in Kentucky, the centre of which was at Bowling Green, and the left at Columbus, and its reverse was a serious disaster to the Confederates.

The department of General Halleck embraced Kentucky in addition to the country west of the Mississippi. In order to hold the Cumberland and Tennessee rivers, which afforded water communication far back into the country in the rear of their line, the Confederates had built a work, known as Fort Henry, on the Tennessee, a little south of the Kentucky border, and another and a stronger work, known as Fort Donelson, on the Cumberland and a little below Nashville. At the solicitation of Brigadier-General U. S. Grant, commanding at Cairo, General Halleck determined to capture these forts, and so break the Confederate line, and compel their army to fall back from Kentucky. Fort Henry was to be first attacked. The fleet of gunboats under Commodore Foote and Grant's troops from Cairo were sent against Fort Henry, which was captured on the 6th of February after a severe bombardment by the gunboats which had ascended the Tennessee. The garrison escaped to Fort Donelson, twelve miles distant across the country.

The loss of Fort Henry compelled the Confederates to evacuate all their positions in Kentucky. General Beauregard fell back from Columbus to Corinth, Mississippi, and General Sidney Johnston slowly retired from Bowling Green upon Nashville, followed by General Buell with a vastly superior force.

After the capture of Fort Henry the gunboats returned to Cairo, and, taking on board supplies and reinforcements for the army, ascended the Ohio and entered the Cumberland, up which they passed to Fort Donelson. Grant in the meantime marched across the country from Fort Henry to Fort Donelson, and invested the latter work. The roads were so difficult that although the distance between the two forts was but twelve miles, Grant spent six days in marching it. This delay gave General Johnston an opportunity to reinforce Fort Donelson. He halted at Nashville with his main army to await the result of Grant's attack on the fort. The gunboats did not join Grant until the 14th of February, and the investment was not begun until their arrival.

ADMIRAL FOOTE.

Fort Donelson was a stronger work than Fort Henry, and was held by a force of about thirteen thousand men, commanded by General John B. Floyd. On the 14th of February the gunboats opened fire upon the fort, and at the same time the army of General Grant, reinforced to about thirty thousand men, began to occupy the positions assigned it in the investment. The operations of the 14th ended with the repulse of the fleet, Commodore Foote being severely wounded in the engagement. Satisfied of his inability to hold the fort against the overwhelming force of the Federal army, General Floyd resolved to cut his way through, and retreat upon Nashville. On the 15th he made a gallant attempt to break through Grant's lines, but was driven back, and a portion of the southern intrenchments remained in the hands of the Union army. On the night of the 15th a council of war was held by the Confederate commanders. It was evident that escape was impossible and a surrender inevitable. General Floyd refused to surrender, and retreated from the fort with a considerable force of infantry and cavalry, with which he succeeded in reaching Nashville. General Pillow, who was left by Floyd in command, turned over the command to General Buckner, the next in rank, and joined Floyd in his flight. Being unable to offer further resistance, General Buckner, on the morning of the 16th, surrendered the fort and his troops unconditionally to the Federal army.

The capture of Fort Donelson was by far the most important success that had yet been won by the Union armies, and was hailed with rejoicings throughout the north and west. By this capture over five thousand prisoners, besides the Confederate wounded, fell into the hands of the Union forces. The Confederates also lost heavily in killed and wounded.

General Johnston, upon learning of the fall of Fort Donelson, fell back from Nashville to Murfreesboro', from which place he subsequently continued his retreat across the State, and eventually joined General Beaure-

NASHVILLE, TENNESSEE.

gard, who had taken position at Corinth, at the junction of two important railway lines on the northern border of Mississippi. Beauregard, in falling back from Columbus, had left a force at Island No. 10, which had been strongly fortified, to hold the Mississippi against the efforts of the Federal fleet and army to obtain the control of the river.

Nashville was occupied by the army of General Buell, and Grant's army was moved up the Tennessee as far as Pittsburg Landing. General Buell was ordered to march across the country from Nashville to the Tennessee, to unite his forces with Grant's, and attack the Confederates at Corinth.

* General Johnston, the Confederate commander, had feared this concen-

51

tration, which would make the Federal power in this quarter irresistible, and had determined to attack Grant's army and crush it before Buell could arrive, after which he would be free to engage Buell. His plan was ably conceived, but his march was delayed by the fearful state of the roads, and he did not arrive opposite the Federal position until two days after the time fixed for his attack. Grant was encamped at Shiloh Church,

near Pittsburg Landing, with the Tennessee river in his rear. On the morning of Sunday, April 6th, his army was suddenly attacked by Johnston, and was driven steadily from its original position to the banks of the Tennessee, where it was sheltered by the fire of the gunboats. The battle was stubbornly contested, and the losses on both sides were very heavy. Late in the afternoon General Johnston was mortally wounded, and died soon afterwards. The command passed

GEN. ALBERT S. JOHNSTON. to General Beauregard, who failed to follow up his advantage. During the night the army of·

General Buell arrived, and reinforced Grant. On the morning of the 7th, Grant attacked the Confederates and after a sharp fight drove them back. They retreated slowly, and returned to Corinth.

While these operations were in progress, the gunboats under Commodore Foote and a strong force of western troops under General Pope laid siege to Island No. 10, on the Mississippi. After a bombardment of twenty-three days, the Confederate works were captured, together with five thousand prisoners, on the morning of the 7th of April, the day on which Beauregard was driven back from Shiloh. The Confederates still held Fort Pillow, a strong work a short distance above Memphis. If this could be captured, the Federal forces would obtain the control of the river as far south as Vicksburg. General Pope was anxious to move against it at once, but his army was ordered to join General Halleck. Commodore Foote being

MAJ.-GEN. D. C. BUELL.

disabled by his wound received at Fort Donelson was succeeded by Captain Davis, who descended the river and took position above Fort Pillow.

General Halleck now repaired to the Tennessee, and took command of the Union armies there, amounting to more than one hundred thousand men. He moved forward leisurely towards Corinth, and laid siege to

·that place. Beauregard, seeing that it was impossible to hold Corinth against this greatly superior force, evacuated it on the night of the 29th of May, and retreated to Tupelo, Mississippi. The next day General Halleck occupied Corinth. The loss of Corinth compelled the evacuation of Fort Pillow, which was abandoned by the Confederates on the 4th of June. On the 6th the Union gunboats descended the river to Memphis and defeated the Confederate flotilla above that city. Memphis at once surrendered, and was occupied by the Union forces. All West Kentucky and West Tennessee were now under the control of the Union armies, which now occupied a line extending from Memphis, through Corinth, almost to Chattanooga.

The Confederates still held East Tennessee in heavy force. Shortly

MEMPHIS, TENNESSEE.

after the evacuation of Corinth General Beauregard was removed from his command, and was succeeded by General Braxton Bragg. Bragg was strongly reinforced, and it was determined to make a bold effort to drive back the Federal advance and regain West Tennessee and, if possible, Kentucky. Bragg's army was concentrated at Chattanooga, and General Kirby Smith at Knoxville was strongly reinforced. Smith was to move from Knoxville, while Bragg was to advance from Chattanooga, and the two armies were to unite in the centre of the State of Kentucky. Their combined forces amounted to over fifty thousand men, and it was hoped that this movement would compel the Federal army to abandon its advance, and fall back into Kentucky to protect that State and Ohio from the Confederates. Then by a decisive victory Bragg expected to be able to overrun and hold Kentucky and even to invade Ohio.

The division of General Smith moved forward about the middle of August, and on the 30th of August defeated a Union force under General Manson at Richmond, Kentucky, inflicting upon it a loss of six thousand

men. Smith then occupied Lexington and Frankfort, and advanced towards Cincinnati ; but ascertaining that a strong force was assembling at that city, under General Lewis Wallace, he fell back to Frankfort, where he joined General Bragg on the 4th of October.

Bragg had begun his march as soon as Kirby Smith had gotten fairly started. His objective point was Louisville, and he hoped to be able to elude the army of General Buell which was at

MAJ.-GEN. H. W. HALLECK. Nashville, and by a rapid advance seize Louisville before Buell's arrival. By the 17th of September he was at Munfordsville, Kentucky, which he captured after several slight encounters, taking forty-five hundred prisoners. Buell in the meantime had divined Bragg's purpose, and had set out from Nashville for the Ohio by forced marches. He reached Louisville before the arrival of the Confederates, and being heavily reinforced advanced to attack Bragg, who had turned aside and occupied Frankfort on the 4th of October. Bragg fell back slowly, ravaging the country along his route; and was followed by Buell with equal deliberation. On the 8th of October an indecisive battle was fought between the two armies at Perryville. After this conflict, in which both sides lost heavily, Buell refrained from attacking Bragg again, and the latter continued his retreat leisurely into Tennessee, taking with him a wagon train forty miles in length, loaded with plunder captured in Kentucky.

GENERAL B. BRAGG.

During this campaign the Federal army under General Grant had held its line in West Tennessee, extending from Corinth to Memphis. A Confederate army under Generals Price and Van Dorn was assembled in Mississippi in front of the Union position. Grant, who was now in command of the Federal forces in West Tennessee (Halleck having been summoned to Washington as commanding General), ordered General Rosecrans to his assistance. Upon the arrival of this

CINCINNATI, IN 1875.

commander with his troops, Grant advanced upon Price at Iuka, and defeated him on the 19th of September.   He then repaired to Jackson, Tennessee, leaving Rosecrans with nineteen thousand men to hold Corinth against the Confederates.

After his defeat at Iuka Price was joined by Van Dorn, whose troops brought the strength of the Confederate army to eighteen thousand men. They at once advanced upon Corinth, and on the 4th of October attacked that place.   The battle which ensued was noted for the obstinacy with which it was contested by both sides.   The Confederates were defeated

LANDING AT LOUISVILLE, KENTUCKY.

with a loss of about three thousand killed and wounded, and were pursued for about thirty miles southward. The Union loss was about five hundred and eighteen killed, wounded, and missing. ·

The Federal government was greatly dissatisfied with Buell's failure to intercept Bragg, and upon his arrival at Nashville he was removed from the command of his army, which was conferred upon General Rosecrans, as a reward for his victory at Corinth.   Bragg had taken position near Murfreesboro', about thirty miles distant from Nashville, and Rosecrans, towards the last of December, moved upon that place to attack him. Bragg had at the same time completed his preparations to resume the offensive, and had begun his advance upon Nashville, and the two armies encountered each other at Stone river, near Murfreesboro', on the 31st of December. They were about equal in strength, each numbering about forty thousand men. The battle was fiercely disputed, but at nightfall Rosecrans was driven back with heavy loss, and Bragg telegraphed to Richmond news of a great victory. Rosecrans, however, had merely fallen back to a new and stronger position. On the 2d of January, 1863, Bragg renewed his attack, but was repulsed with terrible slaughter. On the 3d a heavy rain fell and prevented all military operations, and that night Bragg retreated from the field. He retired in good order to Tullahoma, about thirty miles from Murfreesboro'. The losses on both sides in this battle were heavy, ranging from ten thousand to twelve thousand men in each army.

The Confederates, having lost the upper and lower Mississippi, had fortified Vicksburg and Port Hudson, in order to maintain their hold upon that stream, and to keep open their communications with the country west of the Mississippi. Vicksburg had been made a post of extraordinary strength, and was garrisoned by a considerable force of Confederate troops. Towards the last of the year General Grant determined to undertake an expedition against it. He sent General Sherman, with forty thousand men, and a fleet of gunboats, under Commodore Porter, to descend the Mississippi and attack the southern works above the city; and advanced southward from Corinth with the main army by land. Grant had accomplished fully half the distance when a strong body of Confederate cavalry, under General Van Dorn, made a dash into his rear, and on the 20th of December captured Holly Springs, Grant's principal depot of supplies. This movement compelled Grant to abandon his advance upon Vicksburg, and to fall back and re-establish his communications with his base. Sherman, ignorant of this disaster, left Memphis on the 20th of December, and a few days later landed his troops on the banks of the Yazoo, from which he advanced upon the Confederate works at Chickasaw bayou, on the north of Vicksburg. On the 29th of December he made a spirited attack upon them, but was repulsed. He withdrew his troops to the boats, and retired to Young's Point, on the Louisiana shore, a short distance above Vicksburg.

MAJOR-GENERAL W. ROSECRANS.

The Confederates were driven out of Missouri at the close of 1861, as we have seen, and retired into Arkansas. General Van Dorn was now sent by the Confederate government to take command of the forces of Price and McCulloch, which numbered about sixteen thousand men. He reached the head-quarters of this force on the 3d of March, 1862. The Federal army, under General Curtis, with General Sigel as his second in command, had taken position on the heights of Pea Ridge, around Sugar creek, in the northwestern part of Arkansas. It numbered about eleven thousand men. On the 7th of March Van Dorn attacked the Union army in this position, and after a bloody fight, which lasted for about seven or eight hours, drove it back. Curtis took up a new position dur-

LITTLE ROCK, ARKANSAS.

ing the night, and the next morning the Confederates renewed the attack, and were repulsed. After the battle of Shiloh the troops of Price and Van Dorn were withdrawn across the Mississippi to reinforce General Beauregard at Corinth. We have seen them bearing the brunt of the campaign in northern Mississippi against Grant's army. Towards the close of the summer, it being necessary to make a vigorous effort to hold the trans-Mississippi region against the efforts of the Union forces, the Confederate government sent Lieutenant-General Holmes to take command of it. The operations in this region during the remainder of the year were of an unimportant character.

The plan of the Federal government for seizing the prominent points on the coast was carried forward with great energy during the year 1862.

Between Albemarle and Pamlico sounds, on the coast of North Carolina, lies Roanoke island, famous as the scene of Sir Walter Raleigh's unfortunate attempts to colonize America, and commanding the entrance to Albemarle sound. The possession of this island by the Federal forces would give them the command of the rivers entering into the sounds, place the rear defences of Norfolk at their mercy, and afford them a safe base from which to attack the towns on the North Carolina coast. The Federal government having determined to obtain possession of Roanoke island, a powerful expedition against it was fitted out early in the year, under the command of Major-General Ambrose E. Burnside. The expedition sailed from Hampton Roads on the 11th of January, 1862, and after narrowly escaping being scattered by a severe storm passed through Hatteras inlet, and anchored in Pamlico sound on the 28th. On the 6th of February the fleet took position off Roanoke island, and on the 7th opened fire upon the Confederate works. Under the cover of this fire a force of over ten thousand troops was landed upon the island. On the 8th General Burnside attacked the Confederate intrenchments and carried them after a sharp contest. The entire Confederate force, numbering about twenty-five hundred men, fell into his hands as prisoners of war. On the 10th the Confederate squadron in Albemarle sound was attacked and destroyed, or captured.

Having established himself firmly on Roanoke island, General Burnside prepared to reduce the towns along the coast of North Carolina. On the 14th of March Newberne surrendered to him, and on the 25th of April Fort Macon, at the entrance of Beaufort harbor, one of the strongest works on the coast, capitulated.

Some important successes were won on the coast of Florida during the spring of this year. An expedition from Port Royal captured Fernandina and Fort Clinch on the 28th of February, and a little later Jacksonville, on the St. John's river, and St. Augustine passed into the hands of the Federal troops. Brunswick and Darien, important places on the coast of Georgia, were captured about the same time.

The most important naval expedition of the year was that which resulted in the capture of New Orleans. The Federal government had recognized from the first the importance of regaining possession of the Mississippi, and, as we have seen, a large fleet of gunboats had been prepared on the upper waters of that stream to co-operate with the army in its efforts to capture the fortified posts along the river. All these efforts, however, were useless, as long as the Confederates retained possession of the lower river or of the important city of New Orleans, the commercial metropolis of the south. It was resolved at an early period of the struggle to wrest New Orleans from the Confederates, and a fleet of forty-five vessels of war and mortar-boats was assembled for this purpose, and placed under command of Commodore Farragut, an able and experienced officer. To the fleet was added a force of fifteen thousand troops, under General B. F. Butler. The expedition rendezvoused at Ship island, near the mouth of the Mississippi, in the early part of March.

About twenty miles above the head of the passes of the Mississippi, and about seventy miles below New Orleans, the entrance to the river is defended by two strong works—Fort Jackson on the right bank of the stream, and Fort St. Philip on the left—both built before the war. The Confederates had further strengthened their position by stretching six heavy chains, supported on a series of dismasted schooners, across the river, from shore to shore, to prevent the passage of ships. Early in April the fleet sailed from Ship island, leaving the troops there to await the result of its operations, and entering the Mississippi took position below the forts. On the 18th the bombardment of the forts was begun by the ships and the mortar-boats, and was continued with great vigor until the 24th. The results of this bombardment were most discouraging, and Farragut became convinced that the forts could not be reduced by the fire of the fleet. He therefore determined to pass them with his vessels and so neutralize them.

ADMIRAL FARRAGUT.

The chain and raft barricade across the river had been broken by a severe storm, and Farragut sent a party to enlarge the gap made in it, so as to admit the passage of the fleet. This task was accomplished with great gallantry. At three o'clock, on the morning of the 24th of April, the fleet got under headway and began to ascend the river, the commodore in his flag-ship, the "Hartford," leading the way. The fleet consisted of seventeen vessels, carrying two hundred and ninety-four guns. As the vessels came abreast of the forts the Confederates opened a heavy fire upon them, to which they responded with vigor. The forts were passed in safety at length, and a short distance above them Farragut encountered the Confederate fleet, consisting of sixteen vessels, but eight of which were armed. Two of these were iron-clads, however. A desperate battle ensued, which resulted in the total destruction of the southern fleet. When the sun rose on the morning of the 24th the forts had been passed, and the resistance of the Confederate vessels had been overcome.

There was nothing now between the Federal fleet and New Orleans, and Farragut, ascending the river slowly and cautiously, anchored in the stream, in front of the city, on the morning of the 25th. He at once demanded the capitulation of New Orleans, which had been evacuated by the Confederate troops on the previous day, and the city was surrendered

VIEW IN ST. CHARLES STREET, NEW ORLEANS.

to him by the municipal authorities. On the 28th Forts Jackson and St. Philip surrendered to Captain Porter, the commander of the mortar fleet. New Orleans being taken word was sent to General Butler, at Ship island, to hasten forward with his troops to occupy it. He arrived on the 1st of May, and at once took possession of the city. Baton Rouge, the capital of Louisiana, was occupied by the Federal forces, and Farragut pushed on up the river, and, passing the Confederate batteries at

Grand Gulf and Vicksburg, joined the fleet of Commodore Davis at Memphis.

The capture of New Orleans was a terrible blow to the south. It deprived the confederacy of the largest and wealthiest city within its limits, and wrested from it the whole of the lower Mississippi.

Another success was gained by the Union arms on the southern coast. An expedition from Port Royal, under General Hunter, laid siege to Fort Pulaski, near the mouth of the Savannah river. This fort was constructed by the Federal government previous to the war, and constituted one of the principal defences of the city of Savannah. On the 11th of April, after a bombardment of fifteen days, it surrendered to General Hunter. Its capture closed the Savannah river to the entrance of the class of vessels known as blockade runners, and deprived the south of the use of one of its principal ports.

The events of this year in Virginia were of the highest importance.

The army of the Potomac, nearly two hundred thousand strong, was ready for active operations with the early spring. General McClellan was anxious to avail himself of the superior naval strength of the United States to transport his army to a point on the Chesapeake bay, from which it could easily interpose between the Confederate army, under General Johnston, and Richmond. Suspecting such a

MAJOR-GENERAL B. F. BUTLER. design on the part of McClellan Johnston abandoned his position at Centreville on the 8th of March, and fell back to the Rappahannock, and a little later moved back still farther to the line of the Rapidan. McClellan advanced to Centreville as soon as informed of Johnston's withdrawal, but was too late to interfere with the movements of the Confederate army.

Simultaneous with Johnston's withdrawal from Centreville occurred an incident which forms one of the most striking episodes of the war, and led to results of world-wide importance. Upon the evacuation of the Norfolk navy yard by the Federal forces, at the outset of the war, the splendid steam frigate "Merrimac" was scuttled and sunk. This vessel was subsequently raised by the Confederates, and rebuilt by them. Her upper deck was removed, and she was covered with a slanting roof. Both the roof and her sides were heavily plated with iron, and a long, stout bow was fitted to her to enable her to act as a ram. She was then armed with ten heavy guns, and named the "Virginia." Thus prepared she was the most powerful vessel afloat.

As soon as the "Virginia" was ready for service the Confederate authorities determined to test her efficiency by attempting to destroy the Federal fleet in Hampton Roads. On the 8th of March the "Virginia," accompanied by two small vessels, left Norfolk and steamed down the Elizabeth river into Hampton Roads. Her appearance took the Federal fleet by surprise, and a heavy fire was concentrated upon her from the fleet and the batteries on shore at Newport's News, at the mouth of the James river. Shot and shell flew harmlessly from her iron sides, and, firing slowly as she advanced, she aimed straight for the sloop of war "Cumberland"—the most formidable vessel of her class in the navy—and sunk her with a blow of her iron prow. The frigate "Congress," lying near by, was chased into shoal water and compelled to surrender, after which she was set on fire. The ram then endeavored to inflict a similar fate upon the frigate "Minnesota," but that vessel escaped into water too shallow for the iron-clad to venture into. At sunset the "Virginia" drew off, and returned to the Elizabeth river. She had destroyed two of the finest vessels in the Federal navy, and inflicted upon her adversaries a loss of two hundred and fifty officers and men. She was herself uninjured, and had but two men killed and eight wounded.

The success of the "Virginia" struck terror to the fleet in Hampton Roads, and it was by no means certain that the victorious vessel would not the next day either attack Fortress Monroe, or pass by it

MAJ.-GEN. GEO. B. M'CLELLAN.

and ascend the Chesapeake, in which case both Washington and Baltimore would be at her mercy. During the night, however, a most unlooked-for assistance arrived. The "Monitor," an iron-clad vessel of a new plan, invented by Captain John Ericsson, entered Hampton Roads on her trial trip from New York. Upon learning the state of affairs her commander, Lieutenant Worden, determined to engage the "Virginia" the next day. On the morning of the 9th the "Virginia" again steamed out of the Elizabeth river into Hampton Roads. The "Monitor," though her inferior in size, and carrying but a single gun, at once moved forward to meet her. An engagement of several hours' duration ensued, in which both vessels were fought with great gallantry; and at the end of this time the "Virginia" drew off, and returned to Norfolk severely injured. The arrival of the "Monitor" was most fortunate. It saved the Federal fleet in

Hampton Roads from total destruction, and prevented the "Virginia" from extending her ravages to the ports of the Union. The battle between the "Monitor" and the "Virginia" will ever be famous as the first engagement between iron-clad vessels. It inaugurated a new era in naval warfare. In spite of the result of the battle, however, the presence of the "Virginia" at Norfolk deterred the Federal forces from risking an attack on that place, and prevented them from making any effort to ascend the James river with their fleet.

In the meantime the army of General McClellan had returned to its position near Alexandria, after the retreat of the Confederates to the Rapidan. General McClellan now proposed to move the bulk of his army to Fortress Monroe, and to advance from that point upon Richmond by way of the peninsula between the York and James rivers. About seventy-five thousand men were left on the Potomac to cover Washington, and the remainder, about one hundred and twenty thousand in number, were transported by water to Fortress Monroe. This movement was accomplished by the 2d of April. On the 4th the army of the Potomac began its march towards the lines of Yorktown, which were held by about eleven thousand five hundred men, under General Magruder. The Confederate commander had passed the first year of the war in fortifying his position, and had constructed a series of powerful works which enabled him, with his small force, to hold McClellan's whole army in check. On the 5th and 6th of April McClellan made repeated attempts to force the southern lines, and failing in these decided to lay siege to them. The time thus gained by Magruder enabled General Johnston to move his army from the Rapidan to the peninsula. It was in position on the lines of Yorktown by the 17th of April, making the force opposed to McClellan about fifty-eight thousand strong. The Confederates did not expect to hold their position on the peninsula, but from the first intended to move back nearer to Richmond, and occupy the line of the Chickahominy. When their preparations were completed they fell back from the lines of Yorktown, on the night of the 3d of May, just as McClellan was about to begin his bombardment of their position.

The Federal army discovered the retreat on the morning of the 4th of May, and moved forward promptly in the hope of intercepting the southern army. On the morning of the 5th the advanced forces attacked the rear-guard of Johnston's army at Williamsburg. The Confederate commander held his ground until his trains had gotten off in safety, and then resumed his retreat, and reached the Chickahominy about the 10th of May without further molestation from the Union forces. General McClellan, following leisurely, took position on the left bank of the Chickahominy, with the river between the two armies.

In accordance with General McClellan's urgent request, President Lincoln decided to order the force left to cover Washington to join the army of the Potomac, before Richmond, by way of Fredericksburg. With his force thus augmented the Union commander had no doubt of his ability to capture Richmond. Alive to this danger General Johnston directed General Jackson, who had been left to hold the valley of Virginia, to manœuvre his army so as to threaten Washington, and compel the Federal government to retain the force intended for McClellan for the defence of Washington. While awaiting the arrival of this force McClellan threw his left wing across the Chickahominy, and lodged it in a position nearer to Richmond. The Federal lines now extended from Bottom's Bridge, on the Chickahominy, to Mechanicsville, north of that stream.

The evacuation of the peninsula compelled the Confederates to abandon Norfolk also. They withdrew their troops from that city on the 9th of May, and sent them to reinforce General Johnston. On the 10th Norfolk and Portsmouth were occupied by the Federal forces under General Wool. Before leaving the Confederates had set fire to the navy yard, which was destroyed. The iron-clad steamer "Virginia" was taken into the James river, and on the 11th was abandoned and blown up. The loss of this steamer, which could have held the James against the whole Union fleet, left the river open to within eight miles of Richmond. The gunboats, including the "Monitor," were sent up to try to force their way to Richmond, but on the 15th of May were driven back by a battery of heavy guns located on the heights at Drewry's bluff, eight miles below Richmond. They were badly injured by the plunging fire of the Confederates. The river was securely obstructed at this point to prevent a passage of the batteries by the Federal fleet.

Having been heavily reinforced, General Johnston determined to attack McClellan's exposed left wing, and on the 31st of May fell upon it at Seven Pines, and drove it back with heavy loss. General Johnston was severely wounded towards the close of the day, and was unable to carry out the plan upon which he had begun the battle. The next day there was heavy skirmishing until about ten o'clock in the morning, but nothing of a more serious nature was attempted by either side. General McClellan, warned by the narrow escape of his left wing, now proceeded to fortify his position on the south bank of the Chickahominy.

While these events were in progress on the Chickahominy, General Jackson carried out with brilliant success the movements assigned him in the valley of Virginia. His task required the exercise of the greatest skill and determination. He was to neutralize the forces of Fremont,

Banks and McDowell, and prevent them from rendering any assistance
to McClellan. Jackson's army fell back from Winchester on the 11th of
March, and retired as far as Mount Jackson. Then rapidly retracing its
steps it attacked Banks' forces at Kernstown, near Winchester. Though
repulsed in this engagement, it succeeded in alarming the Federal government for the safety of Washington. Banks' command was therefore retained in the valley to watch Jackson, and the
force under McDowell was not allowed to go to
McClellan's assistance on the peninsula, lest by
so doing it should uncover Washington. After
the battle of Kernstown, Jackson retired up
the valley, and a season of comparative quietude
ensued. The Federal government even believed
that his troops had been sent to Richmond.
Fremont's army was ordered to move from
LIEUT.-GEN. T. J. JACKSON. western Virginia into the valley; Banks was
directed to march to Manassas and cover
Washington; while McDowell, with forty thousand men, was ordered
to move to Fredericksburg, from which he was to march across the
country and unite with McClellan's left wing, which was thrown out far
to the north of Richmond to meet him. These orders were in process of
execution when Jackson, who had been reinforced by a division under
General Ewell, destroyed the whole Federal plan of campaign.

Knowing that he could not possibly resist the combined forces of Fremont and Banks, Jackson determined to beat
them in detail. Marching rapidly westward, he
crossed the mountains, fell upon the advance
guard of Fremont's army at McDowell, on the
8th of May, defeated it, and drove it back into
western Virginia. Then retracing his steps with
remarkable speed, he returned to the valley, and
on the 23d of May attacked Banks' outlying force
at Front Royal, and drove it in upon the
main body at Strasburg. Banks at once   MAJ.-GEN. N. P. BANKS.
broke up his camp, and fell back down the
valley, pursued by Jackson, who dealt him a terrible blow at Winchester on the 25th. By extraordinary exertions Banks succeeded in
escaping across the Potomac, but left about three thousand prisoners, several pieces of artillery, nine thousand stand of arms, and the greater part
of his stores in the hands of the Confederates.

This bold advance greatly alarmed the government at Washington, and the president ordered Fremont to move with speed into the valley, and directed General McDowell to suspend his movement to the assistance of McClellan, and send a force of twenty thousand men to gain Jackson's rear, and prevent his return up the valley. McDowell sent the required force under General Shields, and Fremont hurried on to gain the upper valley in advance of Jackson. These movements entirely prevented McClellan from receiving the assistance of McDowell's corps, and saved Richmond from capture.

Jackson was too good a general to be caught in the trap so skilfully laid for him. He retired up the valley with the greatest speed, and having interposed his army between Fremont and Shields, turned upon the former, and with a part of his force attacked him at Cross Keys on the 8th of June, and checked his advance. Then reuniting his forces he fell upon Shields at Port Republic on the 9th of June, and drove him back with heavy loss after one of the hardest-fought battles of the war. Having thus put an end to the pursuit of his antagonists, Jackson withdrew to a safe position, from which he could hold them in check or go to the aid of the army defending Richmond. The latter move being decided upon, he eluded the Federal forces in the valley, and marched rapidly to the Chickahominy. Before his absence from the valley was suspected, he had joined General Lee. His campaign in the valley is justly regarded as one of the most

BRIG.-GEN. JAS. SHIELDS.

brilliant of the war. With less than twenty thousand men he had neutralized a force of sixty thousand Union troops, and prevented the execution of McClellan's carefully laid plans for the capture of Richmond.

Upon the fall of General Johnston the command of the Confederate army before Richmond was conferred upon General Robert E. Lee, whom subsequent events proved to be the ablest of the southern leaders. Troops were drawn from every possible point to reinforce General Lee's army, and by the middle of June his forces, including Jackson's army, amounted to ninety thousand men. The Federal army was one hundred and fifteen thousand strong. Both armies were in fine condition. General McClellan, finding it impossible to obtain the assistance of McDowell's corps, and fearing for the safety of his communications with his base of supplies, which was at West Point, at the head of the York river, prepared to move his army to the south side of the Chickahominy, and establish a new and more secure base upon the James river. Before he could put this design in operation he was attacked by General Lee, who, on the 25th of June, fell upon the right of the Union line at Mechanics-ville, and forced it back upon the centre at Cold Harbor. On the 26th the position at Cold Harbor was attacked and carried by the Confederates after a desperate struggle. With great difficulty McClellan secured his retreat to the south side of the Chickahominy, and destroyed the bridges in his rear.

Having decided to retreat to the James river rather than attempt to

RICHMOND, VIRGINIA.

retain his communications with West Point, McClellan destroyed his stores, and on the 28th began his retreat from the Chickahominy by way of White Oak swamp. As soon as his movement was discovered pursuit was made by the Confederates, who attacked his rear guard under General Sumner at Savage Station late in the afternoon of the 29th. Sumner held his ground until the darkness put an end to the action, and during the night of the 29th withdrew across White Oak swamp, destroying all the bridges after him. On the 30th General Lee made a last effort to prevent McClellan from reaching the James, and towards the close of the afternoon the bloody battle of Frazier's Farm was fought. It was continued until nine o'clock. The Federal force at Frazier's Farm held its ground until the remainder of McClellan's army had safely traversed White Oak swamp. The object of the battle having been accomplished, McClellan resumed his retreat to the James river, and took position upon Malvern hill, within a short distance of that stream. Here he massed his artillery, and the gunboats in the James river moved up to a point from which they could throw their shells into the Confederate lines. On the afternoon of the 1st of July the Confederates made a gallant attempt to carry Malvern hill, but were repulsed with severe loss. The next morning the Federal army withdrew to Harrison's Landing on the James river. Thus ended the " Seven Days' Battles," during which the Federal army lost about twenty thousand men in killed, wounded and prisoners, fifty-two pieces of artillery, thirty-five thousand stand of arms, and an enormous quantity of stores of all kinds. The Confederate loss was nineteen thousand five hundred and thirty-three killed, wounded and missing.

The retreat of McClellan's army threw the north into the deepest despondency. On the 2d of July President Lincoln issued a call for three hundred thousand fresh troops. The necessities of the struggle, however, made this force insuffi-

MAJ.-GEN. E. V. SUMNER.

cient, and on the 4th of August the president ordered that a draft of three hundred thousand militia should be made and placed in the service of the United States for a period of nine months unless sooner discharged. The States complied with the requisitions upon them, and in the brief period of three months the enormous mass of six hundred thousand fresh troops was raised, armed, and placed in the field.

For the protection of Washington the Federal government now collected the commands of Banks, Fremont and McDowell in one army, and placed it under command of Major-General John Pope, whose capture of Island No. 10 and other points in the west had given him a fair reputation. He assumed his new command with a profusion of boasts, and promised to succeed where McClellan had failed. According to General Pope the capture of Richmond was the easiest undertaking in the world. His army towards the latter part of July advanced to the Rapidan.

To watch this force General Lee, late in July, sent General Jackson's

corps to the Rapidan. On the 9th of August Jackson attacked the advanced corps of Pope's army at Cedar mountain, and defeated it. This .
defeat suspended General Pope's forward movement. General McClellan
now received orders from Washington to evacuate Harrison's Landing and
to reinforce General Pope with his army. He at once put this order in
execution. The withdrawal of his troops was detected by General Lee,
who rapidly reinforced Jackson, and finally moved with his whole army
to the Rapidan. About the same time Burnside's corps, which had been
withdrawn from the southern coast, and was awaiting orders in Hampton
Roads, was directed to move into the Potomac and reinforce Pope. General
Pope had now under his command a force of over one hundred thousand
men. The Confederate army, which was concentrated upon the Rapidan
by the 18th of August, numbered about seventy thousand men. Its
strength was greatly overestimated by General Pope, who deemed it most
prudent to retire behind the Rappahannock, which he did on the 18th
and 19th of August. His new position was well chosen. His right was
at Rappahannock Station, and his left at Kelley's ford, some distance
lower down the river.

General Lee now resolved to attack Pope before he could be joined by
McClellan's troops. He divided his army into two columns, and sent
Jackson's corps by a circuitous route, by way of Thoroughfare gap, to
gain the rear of the Federal army. This daring flank march was accomplished by Jackson, and on the 26th of August he captured Manassas
Junction, Pope's main depot of supplies, with an enormous quantity of
stores of all kinds, and several railroad trains loaded with supplies.
Upon learning of this movement Pope at once fell back from the Rappahannock, intending to crush the isolated corps of Jackson, and at the
same time Lee set off rapidly by way of Thoroughfare gap to join his
endangered lieutenant. Pope's army had been reinforced by the corps
of Porter and Heintzelman, and Reynolds' division of McClellan's army,
and was at least one hundred and twenty thousand strong. He moved
back rapidly to attack Jackson, and encountered Ewell's division near
Manassas Junction on the 27th. Ewell held his ground, and at night
rejoined Jackson, who moved swiftly from Manassas to a new position
near the old Bull Run battle-field. This brought him nearer to Lee, and
secured his retreat in case of a defeat. Ewell's resistance deceived General Pope, who had posted McDowell's and Porter's corps to hold the
road from Thoroughfare gap, by which Lee must advance to Jackson's
assistance. Supposing that Jackson meant to make a stand at Manassas,
Pope ordered these troops to move from the positions they had taken and
to advance upon Manassas Junction. Manassas was reached at noon on

the 28th, and then General Pope saw for the first time how he had been deceived by Jackson, and how he had blundered in leaving the road from Thoroughfare gap open to Lee. He endeavored to repair his error by attacking Jackson at once. He did attack that general in his new position late in the afternoon of the 28th, but was repulsed with severe loss. On the same afternoon General Lee with Longstreet's corps forced the passage of Thoroughfare gap, and bivouacked that night in the open country beyond it. On the morning of the 29th he pushed forward with speed, and by noon his advanced division reached Jackson's position. By four o'clock in the afternoon the Confederate army was reunited under the command of General Lee. About three o'clock in the afternoon General Pope made a heavy attack upon Lee's position, but was repulsed. On the 30th, having reunited all the corps of his army, General Pope determined

GENERAL. R. E. LEE.

to risk the fate of the campaign upon a decisive engagement. The Confederates held a large part of the old battle-field of Bull Run, and the conflict which ensued is usually known as the second battle of Bull Run. It resulted in the defeat of General Pope, who was driven back to the heights of Centreville with heavy loss. On the 31st Jackson attacked the Federal rear-guard at Chantilly. A spirited encounter took place, and the Federal troops were slowly forced back, losing General Phil

Kearney, one of the most accomplished officers in the service. General Pope now withdrew his army within the lines of Washington. He had lost since the opening of the campaign over thirty thousand men, including eight generals killed, thirty pieces of artillery, over twenty thousand stand of arms, and an enormous quantity of stores. The Confederate loss was nine thousand one hundred and twelve, including five generals.

MAJ.-GEN. PHIL KEARNEY. The defeat of the Union army and the presence of the Confederates on the Potomac placed the city of Washington in great danger. The government acted with vigor and decision in this emergency. The losses of Pope's army were made up by reinforcements. General Pope was relieved of his command, and General McClellan was restored to the command of the army of the Potomac. He set to work with energy to reorganize the broken masses of Pope's army into an effective force.

General Lee now crossed the Potomac and invaded Maryland, hoping to be able not only to remove the war from the soil of Virginia, but also to obtain large reinforcements from the southern sympathizers in Maryland. In this he was disappointed, as scarcely any one joined him. On the 5th of September he crossed the Potomac, and on the 6th occupied Frederick City. Harper's Ferry was held by a force of eleven thousand men under Colonel Miles, and it was necessary to reduce this post in order to preserve the communications of the Confederate army with its own country. General Jackson was despatched with his corps to capture Harper's Ferry. He promptly carried the heights overlooking the town, and on the 15th of September the town and garrison surrendered to him after a feeble resistance.

General Lee in the meantime had taken position at South mountain to await the issue of Jackson's attack upon Harper's Ferry. McClellan, advancing slowly from Washington, reached Frederick on the 12th of

MAJ.-GEN. JOHN A. DIX.

September. There he found a copy of General Lee's confidential order to his corps commanders, which had been lost by some one. This document gave the Confederate plan of operations, and enabled McClellan to act with certainty in directing his own movements. Hastening forward he attacked General Lee at South mountain on the 14th of September, and after a stubborn fight Lee fell back behind Antietam creek, and on the morning of the 17th was joined there by the troops of Jackson, who had made a forced march from Harper's Ferry.

The Confederate army numbered about forty thousand men, having been terribly reduced by the straggling of the men on the march through Virginia. The Federal army numbered over eighty thousand men, and was eager for a contest. The prolonged resistance of Harper's Ferry, and the losses of his army by straggling, had defeated Lee's plan of campaign. He was now compelled to retire across the Potomac, and he halted on the Antietam only to secure the reunion of Jackson's corps with his army and a safe passage of the Potomac. On the morning of the 17th of September General McClellan attacked the Confederate army in force, but it held its ground during the day, both armies at nightfall occupying about the same positions they had held in the morning. The Federal loss was twelve thousand four hundred and sixty-nine, including thirteen generals wounded, one mortally; that of the Confederates eight thousand seven hundred and ninety, including three generals killed, five wounded.

The 18th passed quietly away, and that night Lee silently withdrew from his position and retreated across the Potomac. He retired up the valley to Winchester. The Federal army moved to the vicinity of Harper's Ferry, and did not cross the Potomac until the 2d of November.

Upon entering Virginia General McClellan moved towards the Rappahannock with the design of interposing his army between Lee and Richmond. General Lee at once left the valley where he had been detained by the necessity of watching McClellan, and by a rapid march to Warrenton placed his army between Richmond and McClellan. The Federal army continuing to advance, he fell back to Culpepper Courthouse, and McClellan moved forward to the vicinity of Warrenton. On the 7th of November, when about to resume his advance, McClellan, whose conduct of the campaign had not pleased either President Lincoln or the people of the north, was removed from the command of the army of the Potomac, which was conferred upon General Ambrose E. Burnside.

Burnside at once advanced to the banks of the Rappahannock opposite Fredericksburg, intending to pass the river at that place and move upon Richmond. Upon his arrival at Falmouth, opposite Fredericksburg, he found the Confederate army strongly posted on the heights in the rear of the latter place, prepared to dispute his advance. He crossed the Rappahannock on the 11th and 12th of December, and on the 13th attacked the Confederate position, which had been strongly intrenched. He

MAJ.-GEN. A. E. BURNSIDE.

was repulsed with a loss of eleven thousand men, and compelled to retreat across the Rappahannock. This terrible reverse greatly disheartened the army of the Potomac, and destroyed its faith in its commander; and so the year closed gloomily for the Union cause in the east.

In the fall of 1862 President Lincoln took the bold step of issuing a proclamation announcing that if the seceded States did not return to their allegiance to the Union he would declare all the negro slaves within their limits free from the 1st of January next. This proclamation was issued on the 22d of September, immediately after the battle of Antietam. The army and navy of the United States were to enforce the terms of this proclamation, and from the new year there was to be no more slavery within the limits of the Union. The proclamation was avowedly a war measure, but it was sustained by Congress by appropriate legislation during the ensuing winter.

When the year 1862 closed the Federal government, in spite cf its reverses in Virginia, had great cause for hope. It had effected lodgments
of its forces at important points on the southern coast, had captured New
Orleans, the largest and wealthiest city of the south, and had opened the
Mississippi as far as Vicksburg. West Tennessee, Kentucky and northern
Missouri were overrun and held by the Union forces. A decided gain
had been made, and there was reason to hope that the next year would
bring more favorable results. The Confederates were greatly elated,
however, by their successess in the east, which they regarded as counter-
balancing their disasters in the west, and were more than ever resolved
to continue the war " to the bitter end."

CHAPTER XLII.

THE ADMINISTRATION OF ABRAHAM LINCOLN—THE CIVIL WAR—CONCLUDED.

The Emancipation Proclamation—Battle of Chancellorsville—Death of Stonewall Jackson—Invasion of the North by Lee's Army—Battle of Gettysburg—Retreat of Lee into Virginia—Grant's Army crosses the Mississippi—Battle of Champion Hills—Investment of Vicksburg—Surrender of Vicksburg and Port Hudson—Battle of Chickamauga—Rosecrans shut up in Chattanooga—Grant in command of the Western Armies—Battles of Lookout Mountain and Mission Ridge—Defeat of Bragg's Army—The Campaign in East Tennessee—Retreat of Longstreet—Capture of Galveston—Attack on Charleston—Capture of Fort Wagner—Charleston Bombarded—State of Affairs in the Spring of 1864—The Red River Expedition—Grant made Lieutenant-General—Advance of the Army of the Potomac—Battles of the Wilderness, Spottsylvania, and Cold Harbor—Sheridan's Raid—Death of General J. E. B. Stuart—Battle of New Market—Early sent into the Valley of Virginia—Butler's Army at Bermuda Hundreds—Grant crosses the James River—The Siege of Petersburg begun—Early's Raid upon Washington—Sheridan defeats Early at Winchester and Fisher's Hill—Battle of Cedar Creek—The final Defeat of Early's Army—Sherman's Advance to Atlanta—Johnston removed—Defeat of Hood before Atlanta—Evacuation of Atlanta—Hood's Invasion of Tennessee—Battle of Franklin—Siege of Nashville—Hood defeated at Nashville—His Retreat—Sherman's "March to the Sea"—Capture of Savannah—Battle of Mobile Bay—Attack on Fort Fisher—The Confederate Cruisers—Sinking of the "Alabama" by the "Kearsarge"—Re-election of President Lincoln—Admission of Nevada into the Union—The Hampton Roads Peace Conference—Capture of Fort Fisher—Occupation of Wilmington—Sherman advances through South Carolina—Evacuation of Charleston—Battles of Averasboro' and Bentonville—Sherman at Goldsboro'—Critical situation of Lee's Army—Attack on Fort Steadman—Sheridan joins Grant—Advance of Grant's Army—Battle of Five Forks—Attack on Petersburg—Evacuation of Richmond and Petersburg—Retreat of Lee's Army—Richmond occupied—SURRENDER of General Lee's Army—Rejoicings in the North—Assassination of President Lincoln—Death of Booth—Execution of the Conspirators—Johnston Surrenders—Surrender of the other Confederate Forces—Capture of Jefferson Davis—Close of the War.

IN accordance with his proclamation of September 22d, 1862, President Lincoln, on the 1st of January, 1863, issued his proclamation of emancipation, in which he declared all the slaves within the limits of the Confederate States free from that day.

The plan of campaign adopted by the Federal government for 1863 was very much like that of the previous year. In the east the army of the Potomac was to push forward towards Richmond; and in the west the army of General Grant was to capture Vicksburg, and thus open the Mississippi, after which it was to march eastward, unite with the forces of General Rosecrans and occupy East Tennessee, thus cutting the communication between the Border and the Gulf States. In addition to these operations an expedition against Charleston, South Carolina, was to be attempted.

The army of the Potomac was greatly disheartened by its defeat at Fredericksburg, and had lost confidence in General Burnside. That commander, at his own request, was removed from the command, and was succeeded by General Joseph Hooker on the 25th of January. Hooker at once began the reorganization of his army, and soon brought it to a splendid state of efficiency. By the opening of the spring it numbered one hundred and twenty thousand men and four hundred pieces of artillery. General Lee had remained in his position back of Fredericksburg all winter, and his army had been weakened by the withdrawal of General Longstreet's corps, twenty-four thousand strong, by the Confederate government, leaving him about fifty thousand men.

General Hooker, upon learning of Lee's weakened condition, determined to attack him. He divided his army into two columns. One of these, consisting of the Second, Fifth, Eleventh, and Twelfth army corps, under his own command, was to cross the Rappahannock above Fredericksburg and turn the Confederate position. The other column, consisting of the First, Third, and Sixth corps, under General Sedgwick, was to cross the river at Fredericksburg and attack the heights. Between these forces it was believed that Lee's army would be crushed. On the 27th of April Hooker moved off with the first column, crossed the river on the 28th and 29th at Kelley's ford, and on the 30th took position at Chancellorsville, on the left and in the rear of Lee's fortified line. On the 29th General Sedgwick crossed his column about three miles below Fredericksburg, and during that day and the 30th made demonstrations as though he intended to assault the southern position in the rear of the town.

General Lee's situation was now critical, and demanded the most extraordinary exertions of him. Leaving a small force to hold the heights in the rear of Fredericksburg, he moved with his main body towards Chancellorsville, where Hooker had intrenched himself with about eighty thousand men. His only hope of safety lay in defeating this force before Sedgwick's column could arrive to its assistance. On the 2d of May he

MAJ.-GEN. JOS. HOOKER.

sent Jackson's corps to turn the Federal right, and with the remainder of his force deceived Hooker into the belief that he meant to storm the intrenched position of the Federal army. Jackson performed his flank march with success, and on the afternoon of the 2d of May made a fierce attack upon the Federal right, and drove it in upon its centre. In this attack he received a mortal wound, of which he died on the 10th of May. The next day, the 3d, having reunited Jackson's corps with his main force, Lee attacked Hooker at Chancellorsville, and drove him back to the junction of the Rappahannock and Rapidan rivers. He was preparing to storm this new position when he learned that Sedgwick had defeated the force left to hold the heights of Fredericksburg on the 3d of May, and was marching against him. His danger was now greater than ever. Leaving a part of his army to hold Hooker in check, he marched rapidly to meet Sedgwick. He encountered him at Salem heights on the 4th of May, and compelled him to recross the Rappahannock at Banks' ford. Then moving back towards Hooker's position Lee prepared to storm it. General Hooker, however, disheartened by Sedgwick's defeat, withdrew his army across the Rappahannock on the night of the 5th, and returned to his old position on the north side of that stream, having lost twelve thousand men and fourteen pieces of artillery in the battle of Chancellorsville. The Confederate loss was also heavy. Out of an army of about fifty thousand men, ten thousand two hundred and eighty-one were killed, wounded and captured. The victory was dearly bought by the Confederates by the death of Stonewall Jackson, who was worth fully fifty thousand men to their cause. At the moment of his success against the Federal right, he was shot down by his own men, who mistook his escort for a party of Federal cavalry.

MAJ.-GEN. J. SEDGWICK.

The success of the Confederates in Virginia was more than counterbalanced by their reverses in the west and southwest. The southern government, anxious to change the course of the war by a bold stroke, decided to follow up the victory at Chancellorsville by an invasion of the north by Lee's army. This army was reinforced heavily, and by the last of May numbered seventy thousand infantry and artillery, and ten thousand cavalry. General Hooker's army on the other hand had been reduced by desertions and expirations of enlistments to about eighty thousand men, making the two forces about equal.

On the 3d of June, 1863, Lee began his forward movement, and marching through the valley of Virginia, captured Winchester, which was held by General Milroy's command, on the 14th, taking four thousand prisoners, and twenty-nine pieces of cannon. On the 22d of June the Potomac was crossed at Williamsport, and the Confederate army moved towards Hagerstown, Maryland. General Hooker had followed Lee from the Rappahannock, and had manœuvred his army so as to interpose it between the Confederates and Washington. On the 23d the advanced corps of Lee's army under General Ewell occupied Chambersburg, Pennsylvania, and on the 25th and 26th General Hooker crossed the Potomac at Edward's Ferry, and marched to Frederick, Maryland. He was anxious to withdraw the garrison of Harper's Ferry, which had retired from that place to the Maryland heights, opposite the town, but the war department refused to allow him to do so. Hooker thereupon relinquished the command of the army, and was succeeded by Major-General George G. Meade, the senior corps commander, and a soldier of genuine ability. General Lee now moved his army east of the mountains, and directed his advance towards Gettysburg. In ignorance of his adversary's design, General Meade hastened forward to occupy the same point.

LIEUT.-GEN. R. S. EWELL.

The invasion of Pennsylvania by the Confederate army aroused the most intense excitement in the north. President Lincoln called out one hundred thousand militia to serve for six months, unless sooner discharged, and as far north as New York preparations were made to receive the Confederate army with a stubborn resistance should it succeed in penetrating so far. Every effort was made to raise troops and forward them to General Meade in time to be of service to him.

On the morning of the 1st of July the left wing of the army of the Potomac under General Reynolds and the advanced corps of Lee's army under Generals A. P. Hill and Ewell encountered each other at Gettysburg. General Reynolds was forced back and killed. General Hancock was at once sent by General Meade to assume the command of the left wing, and upon his arrival he at once recognized the importance of the position at Gettysburg, and occupied it. He was

MAJ.-GEN. GEO. G. MEADE.

BATTLE OF GETTYSBURG.

promptly reinforced by General Meade, and by the afternoon of the 2d of July the army of the Potomac was securely posted on the heights known as Cemetery Ridge. The Confederate army took position on the opposite hills known as Seminary Ridge. Between the two armies lay the battle-field on which the engagement of the 1st of July was fought. Heavy skirmishing prevailed throughout the day on the 2d, the advantage being with the Confederates. On the 3d of July General Lee made a general attack upon the Federal position on Cemetery Ridge, which, very strong by nature, had been rendered impregnable by intrenchments. His attack was made with determination, and was a splendid exhibition of American courage, which won for his troops the generous admiration of their adversaries; but it was unsuccessful. The grand charge of the Confederates was made in the afternoon, and was repulsed with terrible slaughter. Still Lee's position was so strong, and the morale of his army so unimpaired, that General Meade deemed it best to remain satisfied with

his victory, and not to risk its fruits by an attack upon the Confederate lines. The victory was decisive. It put an end to the Confederate invasion. On the night of the 4th of July General Lee withdrew from Seminary Ridge and retreated to the Potomac, which he crossed on the 13th and 14th without serious opposition from the Federal army. On the 15th Lee moved back to Winchester. The Federal loss at Gettysburg was twenty-three thousand, and that of the Confederates about the same.

MAJ.-GEN. J. F. REYNOLDS.

On the 17th and 18th of July General Meade crossed the Potomac below Harper's Ferry, and moving east of the Blue Ridge, endeavored to place his army between Lee and Richmond. The Confederate commander by rapid marches reached Culpepper Court-house in advance of him, however, and about the 1st of August occupied the line of the Rappahannock. The remainder of the year witnessed but one important operation by the armies in Virginia. In October General Lee made a sudden forward movement for the purpose of throwing his army between Meade and Washington, but the latter eluded him and reached Centreville in safety. Lee then withdrew to the Rapidan, and the army of the Potomac took position on the north side of that stream. Both armies passed the winter there.

In the west and southwest success crowned the Federal arms. At the opening of the year the army of General Grant lay on the Mississippi above Vicksburg, assisted by the fleet of gunboats under Admiral Porter.

VICKSBURG, MISSISSIPPI.

The first three months of the year were passed by the Federal army in a series of movements along the Yazoo river, the result of which was to convince General Grant that Vicksburg could not be taken from that quarter. He therefore determined upon a new and more daring plan of operations. He decided to march his army across the Louisiana shore from Milliken's bend, above Vicksburg, to New Carthage, below that city, and to run his gunboats and transports by the batteries. Should the boats succeed in passing he meant to cross his command to the Mississippi shore, and attack Vicksburg from the rear. By investing the city from the land side his flanks would rest upon and be covered by the Mississippi, and he could re-establish communication between his right wing and his base of supplies at Milliken's bend. The plan was daring in the highest degree, and required the greatest skill and resolution in its execution.

In order to retain their hold upon the Mississippi the Confederates had fortified Vicksburg with great care. Port Hudson, about two hundred and forty miles lower down the river, had also been fortified, but not so strongly as Vicksburg. As long as the Confederates held these points they were able to keep a considerable extent of the river open to themselves and closed to the Union gunboats. Thus they were enabled to cross in safety the enormous herds of beef cattle which they drew from the rich pastures of Texas for their armies east of the Mississippi. A strong force held the works at Port Hudson. Vicksburg was occupied by a large garrison, and was under the command of Lieutenant-General John C. Pemberton, who, with an army of about thirty thousand men, independent of the garrison of Vicksburg, held the country in the rear of that city. Appreciating the importance of defeating the Federal army in this quarter the Confederate government, in the spring of 1863, sent General Joseph E. Johnston to take command of all the forces in Mississippi. It failed to supply him with a proper force of troops, and General Pemberton treated his orders with open defiance.

Grant having completed his preparations moved his army from Milliken's bend to a point on the Louisiana shore, opposite Grand Gulf. On the night of the 16th of April a division of gunboats and transports ran by the Vicksburg batteries, suffering severely from the heavy fire to which they were exposed for a distance of eight miles. On the night of the 22d a second division passed the batteries with similar loss. Once below Vicksburg, however, the boats were safe. They then proceeded to Grant's position on the river below. On the 29th of April the gunboats attacked the batteries at Grand Gulf, but were repulsed. The troops were then marched to a point opposite Bruinsburg, Mississippi, and the gunboats and transports were run by the Grand Gulf batteries. On the 1st of May the Federal army was ferried across to the Mississippi shore, and at once began its march into the interior. Near Port Gibson a part of Pemberton's army was encountered and defeated on the same day. This success compelled the evacuation of Grand Gulf by the Confederates. Grant now boldly threw his army between Johnston's forces at Jackson and Pemberton's army, intending to hold the former in check, and drive the latter within the defences of Vicksburg. On the 14th of May he

JACKSON, MISSISSIPPI.

attacked Johnston at Jackson, the capital of Mississippi, and forced him to retreat northward towards Canton. Then turning upon Pemberton he attacked him at Champion Hills, or Baker's creek, on the 16th, and inflicted a severe defeat upon him. Pemberton withdrew towards the Big Black river, and the next day met a second defeat there. He now retreated within the defences of Vicksburg, which place was promptly invested by Grant's army. On the 19th of May Grant attempted to carry the Confederate position by assault, but was repulsed with heavy loss. The assault was repeated with a like result on the 22d. There remained then nothing but a regular siege. This was pressed with vigor, and the city was subjected to a terrible bombardment, which caused great suffering to the people. While the siege was carried on Johnston's army was held back, and prevented from undertaking any movement for the

53

relief of Vicksburg. At length, reduced to despair by the steady approach of the Union trenches, Pemberton surrendered the city and his army to General Grant on the 4th of July. By this surrender thirty thousand prisoners, two hundred and fifty cannon, and sixty thousand stand of arms, together with a large quantity of military stores, fell into the hands of the Union forces. It was justly esteemed the greatest victory of the war.

While the siege of Vicksburg was in progress General Banks ascended the Mississippi from New Orleans and laid siege to Port Hudson. Upon hearing of the fall of Vicksburg, the Confederate commander surrendered the post and his army of sixty-two hundred and thirty-three men to General Banks, on the 8th of July.

These victories wrested from the Confederates their last hold upon the Mississippi. They created the most intense rejoicing in the Northern and Western States, and a corresponding depression in the south. Being simultaneous with the defeat of the southern army at Gettysburg, they were regarded as decisive of the war: as indeed they were. From this time we shall trace the declining fortunes of the southern confederacy and the gradual but steady re-establishment of the authority of the Union over the Southern States.

After the battle of Murfreesboro', or Stone river, the army of General Rosecrans remained quietly in winter quarters at Nashville and Murfreesboro'. Bragg's army passed the winter at Chattanooga. Towards the last of June Rosecrans moved forward from Nashville, and advancing slowly threatened Bragg's communications with Richmond. The Confederate commander had no wish to emulate the example of Pemberton at Vicksburg, and at once evacuated Chattanooga, on the 8th of September, and retired towards Dalton, Georgia. This movement, which was interpreted by Rosecrans as a retreat, was designed to secure the union with Bragg's army of Longstreet's corps, which had been detached from Lee's army and sent to join Bragg. This junction was effected on the 18th, and other reinforcements arrived from Mississippi. Thus strengthened Bragg suddenly wheeled upon Rosecrans, and on the 19th of September attacked him at Chickamauga. The battle was severe, but indecisive, and was renewed the next day. Towards noon, on the 20th, Rosecrans having greatly weakened the other parts of his line to help the left, which was hard pressed, Longstreet made a furious dash at the weakened part, and in an irresistible attack swept the Federal right and centre from the field. Rosecrans endeavored to stop the retreat, but was borne along in the dense crowd of fugitives. Only the left wing, under the command of General George H. Thomas, remained firm. Had that given way the rout would have been complete; but all through the long afternoon Thomas held on to his position with a grim resolution which nothing could shake. After nightfall he withdrew his corps in good order and retired upon Chattanooga. The Union loss at Chickamauga was sixteen thousand men and fifty-one guns; Bragg's about eighteen thousand men.

Bragg advanced at once upon the defeated army of Rosecrans, which had taken refuge in Chattanooga, occupied the heights commanding the city, and seized the communications of the Federal army with Nashville. Thus closely besieged the Union forces suffered considerably from a scarcity of provisions.

General Rosecrans was now removed from the command of the army of the Cumberland, and General Grant was appointed to the chief command of all the western armies. He at once set to work to extricate the army of the Cumberland, to the command of which General Thomas had succeeded, from its perilous situation. Hooker was sent with twenty-three thousand men from Meade's army to his assistance, and Sherman was ordered to march with the force which had taken Vicksburg along the line of the railway from 'Memphis to Chattanooga. The arrival of these reinforcements soon changed the aspect of affairs. On the 23d of November the army of the Cumberland made a vigorous sortie and drove the Confederates from the important position of Orchard Knob. On the 24th Hooker stormed Lookout mountain, the left of the Confederate line, and carried it after a hard fight. The investment was now thoroughly broken, and the Confederates were confined to Mission Ridge, which had formerly constituted the right of their line. On the 25th this position was assaulted by the whole strength of the Federal army, and was carried after a stubborn fight. Bragg, beaten at all points, with heavy loss, retreated into Georgia, where he was soon after removed from his command and succeeded by General Joseph E. Johnston.

During the progress of this campaign General Burnside had moved from Kentucky with a force of about twenty-five thousand men, about the time that Rosecrans began his advance from Nashville in June. The strong position of Cumberland gap was surrendered to him with scarcely an effort for its defence by the Confederates, and he moved into East Tennessee. Driving back the Confederate forces, which sought to stop his march, he occupied Knoxville. The object of his expedition was to afford a rallying point for the Union men of East Tennessee. After the battle of Chickamauga, and the investment of Chattanooga, President Jefferson Davis visited Bragg's army, and being convinced that the capture of Rosecrans' force was inevitable, decided to withdraw General

CAPTURE OF LOOKOUT MOUNTAIN.

Longstreet's corps from Bragg, and to send it to drive Burnside out of East Tennessee. Longstreet's men were in no condition to undertake such a campaign, but under their energetic commander succeeded in confining Burnside's army to the defences of Knoxville. The siege of that place was formed, and several assaults were made upon the Union works, but were each repulsed with heavy loss. Burnside's men were reduced almost to starvation, but held out with unshaken resolution. After the defeat of Bragg at Mission Ridge Grant ordered Sherman to march with his corps to the relief of Knoxville. Upon the approach of this force Longstreet, on the 4th of December, raised the siege and retreated into Virginia.

Beyond the Mississippi the war was carried on with varying success throughout the year 1863, but to the general advantage of the Federal forces. On the 3d of July the Confederates,

LIEUT.-GEN. J. LONGSTREET.

under General Holmes, attacked Helena, Arkansas, but were repulsed. By the close of the year the Confederate forces had been pressed back as far as the Red river.

On the 1st of January, 1863, Galveston, Texas, which had surrendered to the Federal forces in the fall of 1862, was recaptured by the Confederates, under General Magruder. By the capture of this place the Confederates obtained one more port from which they could maintain communications with and receive supplies from Europe.

In the spring of 1863 a powerful naval expedition, under Admiral Dupont, was despatched against Charleston. On the 7th of April Dupont attempted to force his way into the harbor, but was driven back by the forts and batteries, and nine of his iron-clads were severely injured. Early in July a force of land troops, under General Gilmore, effected a lodgment on the south end of Morris' island, and

ADMIRAL DUPONT.

secured their position by intrenchments. The Union parallels were pushed forward steadily towards Fort Wagner at the north end of the island, and a final assault of that work was ordered. Before the order could be executed Fort Wagner was evacuated on the night of the 6th of September. The Federal batteries on Morris' island now maintained a heavy and constant fire upon Fort Sumter, and reduced it to a shapeless

mass of rubbish on the land side. Yet in this condition it was stronger than at first, the mass of rubbish offering a more effectual resistance to shot and shell than the walls. The long-range guns on Morris' island threw shells into the city of Charleston, which was regularly bombarded from this time until its fall, in 1865. The capture of Fort Wagner enabled the Federal forces to close the harbor of Charleston effectually against blockade runners.

In spite of the victories of Chancellorsville and Chickamauga, and the invasion of the north, the close of the year found the south fairly on the downward road to final failure. Missouri was freed from the presence of the Confederate army, and the greater part of Arkansas was held by the Federal troops. The Mississippi was lost to the south, and

GALVESTON, TEXAS.

the immense supplies from the trans-Mississippi region were no longer available to the Confederate forces east of the great river. Tennessee was occupied by the Federal forces, and the invasion of the north had ended in disaster. The resources of the south were gradually becoming exhausted, and the supply of men was falling off. The north on the other hand was increasing in determination. The war had opened new channels of industry, and these had more than repaid the losses of the first period of the struggle. The north was growing richer, in spite of the war, while the south was growing poorer because of it. At the end of 1863 the Federal debt had reached the enormous total of $1,300,000,000, with the certainty of a heavy increase during the coming year. Still the people of the loyal States responded with heartiness to the heavy demands of the Federal government for men and money. Specie had long since disappeared from circulation, but a system of treasury notes, which were made a legal tender, had replaced coin as a circulating medium. The new paper money was abundant, and the north gave few outward signs of distress. Everything spoke of prosperity. The contrast between the condition of the Union and the confederacy was striking and most suggestive.

Early in the spring of 1864 an expedition was sent into that part of Louisiana known as the Red river country. It consisted of a force of ten thousand troops, under General Smith, from Vicksburg, and a fleet of gunboats, under Admiral Porter. On the 14th of March Fort de Russy was captured by the troops, and on the 21st Natchitoches was occupied. General Banks now arrived with a strong reinforcement of troops from New Orleans, and took command of the expedition. About the 1st of

BRIG.-GEN. Q. A. GILMORE.

April he set out for Shreveport, at the head of navigation on the Red river, his army marching along the shore, and the gunboats ascending the stream. The Confederates gathered in heavy force, under the command of General Kirby Smith, to oppose his advance. On the 8th of April the Confederate army attacked Banks at Sabine Cross-Roads, near Mansfield, and inflicted a stinging defeat upon him. The Union forces were rallied at Pleasant Hill, where they were attacked by the Confederates on the 9th. The Confederates were repulsed, but Banks continued his retreat, and reached Alexandria on the 25th of April. The expedition then returned to the Mississippi. Banks was relieved of the command at New Orleans, and was succeeded by General Canby.

MAJOR-GENERAL E. CANBY.

General Steele, commanding the Union forces in Arkansas, had moved from Little Rock, on the 23d of March, towards Shreveport, to co-operate with General Banks. He was attacked by the Confederates and driven back to Little Rock, which he reached on the 2d of May.

The Red river expedition was thus a total failure, and was a source of great mortification, as well as serious loss, to the Federal government.

Early in March General Grant was raised to the grade of lieutenant-general, that rank having been revived by act of Congress to reward him for his great services during the war. It had been held only by Washington, General Scott having been given only the brevet rank. He was also appointed commander of all the armies of the United States. He decided to assume the immediate direction of the campaign in Virginia, and established his head-quarters with the army of the Potomac. At the same time General W. T. Sherman was appointed to the command of the military division of the Mississippi, in which were included the armies of the Cumberland, of the Ohio, and of the Tennessee. The supreme control of the military operations both east and west was vested in General Grant—a great gain, inasmuch as the operations in the two quarters of the Union could now be made to assist each other. The plan of the campaign embraced a simultaneous advance of both armies; the army of the Potomac was charged with the task of defeating Lee and capturing Richmond; the western army, under Sherman, was to force Johnston back into Georgia.

The army of the Potomac numbered one hundred and forty thousand men on the 1st of May, 1864; the Confederate army, under General Lee, about fifty thousand. General Meade retained the immediate command of the army of the Potomac, but General Grant accompanied it, and directed its movements. On the morning of May 4th—just three days before Sherman moved from Chattanooga—the Federal army crossed the Rapidan, and, turning the right of Lee's position, entered the region known as the Wilderness. General Lee determined to attack this force and prevent it from reaching the open country beyond the Wilderness. On the 5th of May he encountered the army of the Potomac in the Wilderness, near the old battle-field of Chancellorsville. The attack was made by the Federal forces, which endeavored to drive off Lee's army, which blocked the route by which they were advancing. Lee held his ground during the day, and that night both armies bivouacked upon the field. The battle was renewed on the 6th, but Grant failed to force the Confederate position. The fighting during these two days was carried on in a thickly-wooded region, in which the artillery of the two armies could not be used to advantage. On the 6th the Confederates suffered a serious loss in the person of General Longstreet, who was severely wounded. The losses in killed and wounded were very heavy on both sides, as the fighting was of a desperate character.

On the 7th General Grant moved his army around Lee's right, and marched rapidly to seize the strong position of Spottsylvania Court-house, which would have placed him between the Confederates and Richmond. Lee at once divined his purpose, and fell back rapidly to the heights around Spottsylvania Court-house, which he occupied on the

8th. Upon arriving before this position Grant found his enemy strongly intrenched in it, and at once resolved to drive him from it. On the 10th of May he made a determined attack upon the Confederate line, but failed to carry it. At daybreak on the 12th a furious assault was made by Hancock's corps upon the right centre of Lee's line, which was carried in handsome style. Grant at once followed up Hancock's success by vigorous attacks upon the other part of the southern line; but Hancock was unable to advance beyond the works he had captured in his first attack, and the other assaults were repulsed by the Confederates. It was evident that the Confederates could not be dislodged from their position without a still heavier loss to the Union army, and General Grant determined to draw them from the heights of Spottsylvania by another flank march to the right. The losses of the Union army since the opening of the campaign had been enormous, but undismayed by them, General Grant wrote to the war department, after the battle of the 12th of May : " We have now ended the sixth day of very heavy fighting. The result to this time is very much in our favor. . . . I propose to fight it out on this line, if it takes all summer."

On the 21st of May the army of the Potomac moved from Spottsylvania to the banks of the North Anna river, and reached that stream on the 23d. Lee had marched rapidly by a shorter route, and his army was in position on the south side of the river when Grant reached the northern shore. Lee had chosen a position of very great strength in front of Hanover Junction, and had covered it with earthworks. On the 25th Grant crossed a large part of his force to the south side of the North Anna, and endeavored to force the Confederate lines, but discovering its remarkable strength, withdrew his troops to the north shore, and on the 26th moved around Lee's right in the direction of the Chickahominy. Lee followed him promptly and took position at Cold Harbor, on the north side of the Chickahominy, and within nine miles of Richmond, occupying very much the same position held by McClellan's army in the battle of Cold Harbor, on the 27th of June, 1862. He covered his entire line with strong earthworks. On the 1st of June a sharp encounter occurred between the Federal right and the Confederate left wings, and on the morning of the 3d of June Grant made a general assault upon the Confederate works. The attack was made with great gallantry, but was repulsed with a loss to the Federal army of thirteen thousand men. The losses of the army of the Potomac since the passage of the Rapidan had reached the enormous total of over sixty thousand men. The Confederate loss during the same period was about twenty thousand. Failing to force the Confederate line at Cold Harbor, General Grant drew off

BATTLE OF SPOTTSYLVANIA COURT-HOUSE.

leisurely towards the James river at Wilcox's Landing, intending to cross that river and attack Richmond from the south side of the James.

In the meantime, upon reaching Spottsylvania Court-house, General Grant had sent General Sheridan, with ten thousand cavalry, to destroy the railroads connecting Richmond with Lee's army and the valley of Virginia. Sheridan executed his orders with complete success, and went within seven miles of Richmond. On the 10th of May he reached Ashland. He was attacked there by the Confederate cavalry under General Stuart, and moved off towards Richmond. Stuart, marching by a shorter route, threw his cavalry between Sheridan and Richmond, and again encountered him at the Yellow Tavern, on the Brook turnpike, seven miles from the city. Stuart was mortally wounded, and Sheridan secured his retreat across the Chickahominy and down the peninsula. In General Stuart the Confederates lost their only great cavalry leader. Had Sheridan, instead of halting at Ashland, pushed straight on to Richmond, the Confederate capital must have fallen into his hands. On the 25th of June he rejoined General Grant.

At the opening of the campaign General Butler, with a force of about thirty thousand men, known as the army of the James, was sent up the James river to attack the defences of Richmond on the south side of that river. He occupied City Point and Bermuda Hundreds on the 5th of May, and

MAJOR-GENERAL W. S. HANCOCK.

a few days later advanced up the neck of land lying between the James and the Appomattox rivers. To oppose him the Confederates collected a force of about eighteen thousand men under General Beauregard, and posted them in a fortified line extending from the James to the Appomattox, in front of the Richmond and Petersburg railroad. On the 16th of May Butler's army, having advanced within a short distance of this line, was attacked by the Confederates and driven back to Bermuda Hundreds. The Confederates then formed their lines across the narrow peninsula, and kept Butler's force enclosed between their works and the two rivers until the crossing of the James river by the army of the Potomac.

The Federal plan of campaign also included the seizure of the valley of Virginia, and of the railway connecting Virginia with East Tennessee and Georgia. On the 1st of May General Sigel, with an army of ten thousand men, advanced up the valley towards Staunton. On the 15th he was defeated with considerable loss by the Confederates under General Breckenridge at New Market, and was driven back down the valley. General Hunter was appointed in Sigel's place, and succeeded in forcing his way to the vicinity of Lynchburg. Lee, becoming alarmed for the safety of that place, sent General Early, with twelve thousand men, to its assistance. Early at once attacked Hunter, and forced him to retreat by a circuitous route into West Virginia.

MAJ.-GEN. BRECKENRIDGE.

In the meantime General Grant had reached the James river, where his army was reinforced to one hundred and fifty thousand men. On the 15th and 16th of June he crossed his troops near City Point, and advanced upon Petersburg. At the same time General Butler moved forward with the army of the James against the southern works between the James and Appomattox. On the 16th, 17th, and 18th, Grant made repeated attempts to storm the Confederate works before Petersburg and south of the James, but was repulsed with a total loss of nine thousand six hundred and sixty-five men. Being unable to carry the southern works by storm, he began the siege of Petersburg. His right rested on the James above Bermuda Hundreds, and from this point his line extended across the Appomattox, with his left thrown out towards the Weldon railroad. During the summer and fall he continued to extend his left until he had seized the Weldon road.

From this point he sought to extend his left still farther and to seize the South Side railroad, Lee's only remaining line of communication with the south and southwest. Frequent encounters occurred between the two armies during the summer and fall, a number of which attained the proportions of battles, but we have not space to relate them all. On the 30th of July a mine was sprung under one of the principal works of Lee's line, and the explosion was followed by an assault by Burnside's corps. The attack was re-

MAJOR-GENERAL HUNTER.

pulsed with a loss of over five thousand men to the Union troops. During the early autumn General Grant extended his lines across the James river, and established a force on the north side of that river to lay siege to the defences of Richmond. The right of this force was extended as far as the Williamsburg road. This was the situation of the two armies at the close of the year.

In the meantime Early had advanced into the valley of Virginia after the defeat of Hunter. The retreat of that commander into West Virginia had left the Potomac unguarded, and Washington City exposed to attack. General Lee at once reinforced Early to fifteen thousand men, and ordered him to cross the Potomac and threaten Washington, hoping by this bold movement to compel Grant to weaken his army for the protection of the capital, if not to raise the siege of Petersburg. Early moved rapidly, crossed the Potomac near Martinsburg on the 5th of July, and on the 7th occupied Frederick City in Maryland. On the 9th he defeated a small force under General Lewis Wallace at Monocacy Bridge, and advanced upon Washington. The Nineteenth army corps of the Federal army was at Fortress Monroe, where it had just arrived from New Orleans, *en route* to join Grant's army. It was at once ordered to Washington, which, until its arrival, was held by a small garrison, and Grant at the same time embarked the Sixth corps, and sent it with all speed around to the Potomac. These troops reached Washington before the arrival of Early, who appeared before the defences of that city on the 11th of July. He found the works too strongly manned to be attacked by his force. After skirmishing for several days before them, he withdrew across the Potomac on the 14th, and retreated to the neighborhood of Winchester.

MAJ.-GEN. LEW WALLACE.

Early's movement so alarmed the Federal government for the safety of Washington that a force of forty thousand men, ten thousand of which were the splendid cavalry of Sheridan, was stationed in the valley, and Major-General Sheridan was appointed to the command of this army. Had Grant been able to retain these troops with his own army, it is safe to say that Lee would have been forced to abandon his position at Petersburg in the autumn of 1864. Their absence in the valley enabled the Confederate leader to prolong his defence through the winter.

As soon as he had gotten his forces well in hand, Sheridan advanced upon Early, and on the 19th defeated him at Winchester, and drove him back to Fisher's Hill, where, on the 22d, he again defeated him and drove him out of the valley, pursuing him as far as Staunton. By the orders of General Grant, General Sheridan now laid waste the entire valley of the Shenandoah, destroying all the crops, mills, barns, and farming implements, and driving off the cattle with his army as he moved back.

Early was reinforced after his retreat to the upper valley, and about the middle of October, advanced down the valley towards the Federal position with a force of nine thousand men and forty pieces of cannon. The Union army lay at Cedar creek, and was under the temporary command of General Wright during the absence of General Sheridan. On the 19th of October Early attacked this force, and drove it back for several miles.   Instead of continuing the pursuit, his troops stopped to plunder the Federal camp, which had fallen into their hands.   General Wright rallied his men and re-formed them in a new position, and at this moment General Sheridan arrived on the field.   He had heard the firing at Winchester, "twenty miles away," and had ridden at full speed from that place to rejoin his army.   He at once ordered it to advance upon Early, whose men, laden with the plunder of the captured camp, were driven back with terrible force and pursued up the valley for thirty miles.   This success cleared the valley of the Confederate forces, for Early was not able after this to collect more than a handful of men, and Lee had no troops to spare him.   Sheridan's brilliant victories cost him a total loss of seventeen thousand men.

MAJ.-GEN. PHIL SHERIDAN.

The western army under General Sherman was increased to one hundred thousand men, and was concentrated in and around Chattanooga about the last of April.   Opposed to this force General Joseph E. Johnston had collected an army of fifty thousand men at Dalton, Georgia.   The objective point of Sherman was Atlanta, Georgia, the key to the railroad system of the south.

On the 7th of May the Federal army began its advance.   The position at Dalton being too strong to be assaulted, Sherman turned it by a flank movement upon Resaca, to which place Johnston fell back.   On the 14th

GEN. W. T. SHERMAN.

and 15th of May Sherman endeavored to force the Confederate lines near Resaca, but without success.   He therefore moved around Johnston's left again, and compelled him to fall back to Dallas.   Severe fighting occurred on the 25th at New Hope Church, but Johnston maintained his position.   Heavy skirmishing ensued until the 28th, when Sherman having turned Allatoona pass, Johnston occupied a new position, embracing Pine, Lost, and Kenesaw mountains. Between the 15th of June and the 2d of July Sherman made several attempts to force this position, which was one of the strongest yet occupied by the Confederates, and failing to carry it, again moved to the left and turned it. Johnston at once fell back across the Chattahoochee and within the lines of Atlanta.

He had prepared this city for a siege, and had strongly fortified it. He had his army well in hand, and he was determined as soon as the Federal army had passed the Chattahoochee to attack Sherman and force him to a decisive encounter. He hoped to defeat him, and had purposely avoided a general battle until now. Should he succeed in his attempt the defeat of the Federal army at such a great distance from its base might result in its ruin, and at all events would be decisive of the campaign. At this juncture, however, he was removed from his command on the 17th of July by the Confederate

GEN. JOS. E. JOHNSTON.

president, who was greatly dissatisfied with the results of the campaign, and who, it was generally believed, was influenced by his personal hostility to Johnston. General John B. Hood, a gallant soldier, but unfit for the great task imposed upon him, was appointed to succeed General Johnston. In Johnston General Sherman had recognized an antagonist of the first rank, and had conducted the campaign accordingly. He regarded the appointment of General Hood as greatly simplifying the task before him. The Federal army had already paid the heavy price of over thirty thousand men for its advance to Atlanta, while Johnston had lost less than eight thousand men. The conditions were now to be reversed.

MAJ.-GEN. M'PHERSON.

On the 17th of July the Union army crossed the Chattahoochee, and advanced towards Atlanta. On the 20th and 22d Hood attacked the Federal lines on Peach Tree creek, but only to be beaten back with a loss of over eight thousand men, without inflicting any serious injury upon the Union army, which, however, lost General McPherson, one of its ablest commanders. Sherman now drew in his lines closer to Atlanta, and by a skilful movement thrust his army between the two wings of Hood's forces, thus exposing them to the danger of being beaten

in detail. This movement sealed the fate of Atlanta, which was evacuated by the Confederates on the 31st of August. On the 2d of September Sherman occupied the city. Hood retreated towards Macon. The
loss of Atlanta was a serious blow to the south. It placed the Federal
army in the heart of Georgia, and destroyed the principal source from
which the Confederate armies were supplied with military stores, which

GEN. JOHN B. HOOD.

had been manufactured in great quantities at
Atlanta. Rome, Georgia, which was captured
by Sherman's army during the campaign, was
also largely engaged in the manufacture of arms
and ammunition.

General Sherman was now anxious to march
his army through Georgia, and unite with the
Union forces on the coast, but he was unable as
yet to undertake this movement, as Hood with
an army of thirty-five thousand men lay in his
front, and his communications with Chattanooga
and Knoxville were exposed to the raids of the Confederate cavalry. He
now learned that the Confederate government had ordered General Hood
to invade Tennessee for the purpose of drawing his army out of Georgia,
and concluded to make no effort to prevent this movement. The task of
watching Hood was confided to the army of
the Tennessee, under General George H.
Thomas, who was given a sufficient force to
hold Tennessee, and Sherman set about preparing his army for his march to the sea.
Thomas was heavily reinforced from the
north.

Hood began his forward movement towards the last of October, and on the 31st of
that month crossed the Tennessee near Flor-
ence. He remained on this river until the
middle of November, and on the 19th
marched northward, forcing back the command of General Schofield, and effecting a
passage of Duck river on the 29th. Scho-

MAJ.-GEN. GEO. H. THOMAS.

field fell back to Franklin, eighteen miles south of Nashville. He was
attacked on the 30th by the Confederates and forced back to Nashville,
within the defences of which city General Thomas had collected an army
of about forty thousand men. Hood invested the city, and hastened forward his preparations to assault the Federal works. General Thomas,

however, anticipated him, and on the 15th of December attacked the Confederate army and forced it back at all points. The next day, the 16th, the battle was renewed, and Hood was completely routed. On the 17th the Union army set out in pursuit of Hood's broken columns, and followed them for over fifty miles. But for the gallantry of a small rearguard, which preserved its discipline and covered the retreat to the last, the Confederate army would have been scattered beyond all hope of reunion. Hood recrossed the Tennessee with barely twenty thousand men out of the thirty-five thousand with which he had begun the campaign. He had lost half of his generals, and nearly all of his artillery. He fell

SAVANNAH, GEORGIA.

back to Tupelo, Mississippi, and on the 23d of January, 1865, was, at his own request, relieved of his command.

In the meantime General Sherman, leaving Thomas to deal with Hood, had begun his march through the State of Georgia. Satisfied that the war was practically decided in the southwest, he proposed to march to the sea near Savannah, and thence through the confederacy to the position of General Grant's army. This movement would compel the Confederates to mass their forces in his front, and would confine the decisive opera-

54

tions of the war to the country between his own and Grant's armies, between which it was believed the southern forces could be crushed. Everything being in readiness, Sherman cut loose from his communications with Chattanooga and set fire to Atlanta. On the 14th of November he set out on his " March to the Sea," at the head of a splendid army of sixty thousand men. He ravaged the country as he went, leaving behind him a broad belt of desolation, sixty miles in width and three hundred in length. The Confederates had not sufficient force to offer serious opposition to his march, and in about four weeks he reached the coast near the mouth of the Savannah river. On the 13th of December he stormed and captured Fort McAllister, which commanded that river. The city of Savannah was thus left at Sherman's mercy, and was occupied by his army on the 22d of December. By this successful march to the sea, General Sherman had not only gotten his army in a position to co-operate with Grant in the final struggle of the war, but had struck terror to the south. The most hopeful Confederate now saw that the triumph of the Union cause was inevitable and close at hand.

MAJ.-GEN. O. O. HOWARD.

During the year important operations had been undertaken by the Federal forces on the coast. In July a powerful fleet under Admiral Farragut, accompanied by a strong force of troops under General Granger, was sent against Mobile. This city was one of the principal ports of the confederacy and was strongly fortified. The entrance to the bay was commanded by Forts Morgan and Gaines, two powerful works built before the war, and a number of batteries, and a Confederate fleet under Admiral Buchanan—who had commanded the "Virginia" in her fight with the "Monitor"—lay beyond the forts ready to contest the possession of the bay. On the 5th of August Farragut passed the forts with his fleet with the loss of but

ADMIRAL PORTER.

one iron-clad, and entered Mobile bay. He immediately attacked the Confederate fleet, the flag-ship of which was a powerful iron-clad ram— the "Tennessee." After one of the most desperate fights in naval annals, the entire fleet was destroyed or captured by the Union vessels. Fort Powell was evacuated and blown up by its garrison on the same day. On

the 7th of August Fort Gaines surrendered to General Granger, and on the 23d Fort Morgan also capitulated. These successes made the Federal forces masters of Mobile bay, and closed the port to blockade runners; but the city, which was strongly fortified, was not taken until the next year.

Wilmington, on the Cape Fear river, was now the only port in the confederacy remaining open to blockade runners. It was defended by Fort Fisher, an unusually formidable work near the mouth of the Cape Fear. A larger fleet than had yet been employed during the war was assembled in Hampton Roads under Admiral Porter. A force of eight

THE LANDING AT MOBILE, ALABAMA.

thousand troops under General Butler was embarked, and the expedition sailed to the Cape Fear. Fort Fisher was subjected to a vigorous bombardment, which was begun on the 24th of December, and the troops were landed; but at the last moment General Butler decided that the fort was too strong to be assaulted, and the expedition returned to Hampton Roads.

Since the opening of the war the Confederate cruisers had nearly driven the commerce of the Northern States from the ocean. These vessels were built in England, and were usually manned by crews of English seamen under Confederate naval officers. One of these, the "Florida," put to sea in the summer of 1862, and succeeded in reaching Mobile in August of that year. In January, 1863, she ran the blockade, and in three months captured and destroyed fifteen merchant vessels. She was at length seized in the harbor of Bahia, in Brazil, by a Federal man-of-war, and taken to Hampton Roads. The Brazilian government, resenting this breach of its neutrality, demanded the release of the "Florida," but while the negotiations were in progress, she was sunk in Hampton Roads by a collision with another vessel.

The most famous of all the Confederate cruisers was the "Alabama." She was built at Liverpool, and was suffered to go to sea in spite of the protest of the American minister at London. She was commanded by Captain Raphael Semmes, and during her long career captured sixty-five merchant vessels, and destroyed over ten millions of dollars worth of property. During her entire career she never entered a Confederate port. In the summer of 1864 she put into the harbor of Cherbourg, in France,

ADMIRAL WINSLOW.

and was blockaded there by the United States war-steamer "Kearsarge," Captain Winslow. The French government ordered the "Alabama" to leave Cherbourg, and she went to sea on the 19th of June. She was at once attacked by the "Kearsarge," and was sunk by the guns of that steamer after an engagement of an hour and a quarter. Semmes was saved from drowning by an English yacht that had witnessed the battle and was set ashore. The destruction of the "Alabama" was hailed with delight throughout the north.

In the fall of 1864 the presidential election was held in the States remaining faithful to the Union. The Republican party nominated President Lincoln for re-election, and Andrew Johnson, of Tennessee, for the vice-presidency. The Democratic party supported General George B. McClellan for the presidency, and George H. Pendleton, of Ohio, for the vice-presidency. Mr. Lincoln received at the polls 2,213,665 votes to 1,802,237 cast for McClellan; and the electoral votes of every State save those of New Jersey, Delaware, and Kentucky, were cast 'for him.

On the 31st of October, 1864, Nevada was admitted into the Union as a separate State.

The year 1864 closed brilliantly for the Union cause. Though the Confederates had gained a number of important victories during the year, they had, on the whole, steadily lost ground. Virginia, Tennessee, Georgia, Alabama, Mississippi, and Florida were overrun by the Federal armies, and on the coast there was not a single port remaining open to the Confederacy save that of Wilmington, which was blockaded by a powerful fleet. It was evident that the coming spring campaign would end the war. The Federal forces had been increased to the enormous total of one million of men. The Confederates could bring into the field scarcely two hundred thousand men, and for these it was difficult to find subsistence. The vicious financial system adopted by the Confederate government had run its appointed course, and the notes of the Confederate treasury were worth scarcely three or four cents in the dollar.

The year 1865 opened with an effort to secure the return of peace without further bloodshed. In January Mr. F. P. Blair, Sr., came from Washington to Richmond, and on his own responsibility proposed to the Confederate government the appointment of commissioners to negotiate with the Federal government for the close of the war. The following commissioners were appointed by the Confederate government: Alexander H. Stephens, vice-president of the Confederate States; R. M.T. Hunter, senator from Virginia in the Confederate Congress, and John A. Campbell, assistant secretary of war. They proceeded to City Point under a safe conduct from General Grant, and were conveyed from that place to Hampton Roads in a government steamer. On the 3d of February President Lincoln and Secretary Seward having reached Hampton Roads, an informal conference was held between the president and the commissioners. The president refused to entertain any propositions which were not based upon the unconditional submission of the Southern States to the authority of the Union, and as the commissioners had no authority from their government to enter into any such arrangement, the conference accomplished nothing.

BRIG.-GEN. A. TERRY.

In the meantime, however, Admiral Porter, undaunted by the failure of Butler to take Fort Fisher, had remained off the fort with his fleet and had asked for troops to renew the attempt. The same force that Butler had commanded, with fifteen hundred additional men, was placed under General Terry's command and ordered to join Porter. This force arrived off Fort Fisher on the 12th of January, and on the morning of the 13th accomplished its landing with success. A terrible fire was rained upon the fort by the fleet during the 13th and 14th, and on the 14th a daring reconnoissance of the Union force revealed the fact that the fort had been severely damaged by this bombardment. The trenches of the Union army were pushed rapidly through the sand to within two hundred yards

of Fort Fisher in order to attract the attention of the garrison, and on the
15th a feint was made by a force of sailors and marines from the fleet in
this direction.   At the same time the troops under General Terry stormed
the fort from the land side, and after a hard hand-to-hand struggle of
about five hours, during which each traverse was carried in succession by
a separate fight, Fort Fisher was captured.   On the 16th and 17th the

Confederates blew up their other works at the
mouth of the Cape Fear and retreated towards
Wilmington.   The mouth of the river was now
in the possession of the Federal forces, and the
last port of the south was closed.   A number of
blockade runners, ignorant of the capture, ran into
the river and fell into the hands of the victors.
Later in the month, General J. M. Schofield was
placed in command of the department of North
Carolina, and on the 22d of February occupied the
city of Wilmington with his troops.

BRIG.-GEN. SCHOFIELD.

Sherman, after the capture of Savannah, allowed
his army a month's rest on the coast, and towards the end of January
moved northward through South Carolina towards Virginia.   His force
was sixty thousand strong and moved in four columns covering a front
of fifty miles.   His route was marked by the same desolation he had spread
through Georgia.   The roads were in a horrible condition, and in many
places the men were forced to wade through the icy waters up to the arm-
pits.   Still he pressed on right into the heart of the
confederacy.   On the 17th of February he reached
Columbia, South Carolina, having destroyed the
railroad leading north from Charleston.   General
Hardee, commanding the Confederate forces at
Charleston, apprehensive of being shut up in that
city, which was utterly unprepared for a siege,
evacuated Charleston and its defences on the 17th
of February and retreated northward to join General
Johnston in North Carolina.   The next day

LIEUT.-GEN. W. HARDEE.

Charleston was occupied by the Federal forces.
Fort Sumter was also taken possession of at the same time.   The fort
was a mass of ruins; the city was not much better off.   It had suffered
severely from the bombardment to which it had been subjected since
the fall of Fort Wagner, and the Confederates upon their withdrawal had
set fire to a considerable part of it.

From Columbia, Sherman moved towards Fayetteville, North Carolina, driving back the Confederate forces that resisted his progress, and entered that place on the 12th of March. From Fayetteville he moved towards Goldsboro'.

The Confederate government, in the emergency to which it was reduced, was obliged to reappoint General Joseph E. Johnston to the command of the force assembling in Sherman's front. Johnston succeeded in collecting about thirty-five thousand troops, with which he attacked Sherman at Averasboro' on the 16th of March, and again at Bentonville on the 19th. The Confederates fought with their old enthusiasm in these encounters, but were unable to stay the progress of the Federal army, and on the 23d of March Sherman occupied Goldsboro'. Johnston withdrew towards Raleigh. At Goldsboro' Sherman was joined by the forces of Generals Schofield and Terry which had come up from the coast.

MAJOR-GENERAL H. G. WRIGHT.

The armies of Grant and Lee had lain confronting each other during the winter. General Lee had little hope of maintaining his position after the opening of hostilities. His army was growing weaker from sickness and desertion, and no more men could be obtained. The Confederate Congress made a feeble effort during the winter to enlist negro troops in its service, but with a singular recklessness refused to offer the boon of freedom to such of the blacks as would take up arms. That body believed that the negroes would fight for their own enslavement.

Early having been driven out of the valley, General Sheridan was ordered to start from Winchester with a column of ten thousand cavalry, and cut the communications of Lee's army by railroad and telegraph north and east of Richmond. He left Winchester on the 27th of February, and defeating Early's small force at Waynesboro', broke the Virginia Central railroad at that point and moved to Charlottesville, which surrendered to him. He then divided his force into two columns and resumed his "ride" on the 6th of March. He thoroughly destroyed the railroad between Charlottesville and Lynchburg for about forty miles, and the canal between Richmond and Lynchburg shared the same fate for a considerable distance. Being

MAJOR-GENERAL WARREN.

unable to cross the James above Richmond on account of the high water, he moved around the north of Richmond, crossed the river at Deep Bottom, and joined Grant before Petersburg on the 26th of March. He had utterly laid waste the country along his route. The arrival of this splendid force of cavalry was of the greatest service to Grant, as we shall see.

The situation of General Lee's army was growing more critical every day. He had less than forty thousand troops. He was fully convinced of the necessity of abandoning Richmond and Petersburg, and was anxious to do so at once, and unite his army with that of General Johnston and occupy a new position in the interior of the south. In order to secure the withdrawal of his army he determined to make a vigorous attack upon Grant's right, hoping to compel him, in order to help his right, to draw back his left wing, which was in dangerous proximity to the road by which Lee wished to retreat. Could he succeed in this effort, he meant to evacu-

ate his position at Petersburg and retire towards Danville, where he hoped to unite with General Johnston. On the 25th of March he made a heavy attack upon Fort Steadman on the right of Grant's line, and captured it. The Federal forces rallied, however, and drove the Confederates from the captured works back to their own line, inflicting upon them a loss of three thousand men. Lee had now no alternative but to await the movements of General Grant, as he could not afford to make the sacrifice of men which a renewal of his efforts would require of him.

LIEUT.-GEN. A. P. HILL.

General Grant lost no time in taking the field. By the last of March his army, numbering about one hundred and seventy thousand men, including Sheridan's magnificent cavalry division, was in readiness to begin the campaign. On the 29th of March the advance of the Federal army was begun. Leaving the bulk of his army before Petersburg, Grant sent a column of twenty-five thousand men to turn the Confederate right and seize the Southside railroad, Lee's only means of communication with Johnston's army and the country in his rear. By the morning of the 30th the Federal left had gotten fairly to the right of the Confederates. On the 30th a heavy storm prevented a further advance, and Lee took advantage of the delay to reinforce his right wing with all the troops he could spare. On the 31st he attempted to drive back the Federal left, but without success. While this battle was going on, Sheridan swung around the Confederate right and seized the important position of Five

Forks. Lee then sent Pickett's and Johnston's divisions to recover this point, and they drove off the cavalry, and occupied Five Forks at night-fall on the 31st. Being joined by the Fifth corps, Sheridan attacked the Confederates on the morning of the 1st of April, and defeated them after a determined encounter, taking over five thousand prisoners.

As soon as Sheridan had secured Five Forks, Grant opened a heavy artillery fire upon the lines of Petersburg along his whole front, and continued the bombardment through the night. On the morning of the 2d of April he made a determined attack upon Lee's line, and broke it at several points. General Lee was now forced to assume a new and shorter line immediately around Petersburg. The Federal army made a vigorous effort to force its way into the city, but was unsuccessful.

The fate of Petersburg was now decided. It was impossible to hold it longer. On the night of the 2d of April General Lee withdrew his army from Richmond and Petersburg, and retreated in the direction of Amelia Court-house. His intention was to move towards Danville, and endeavor to join Johnston. His retreat was discovered on the morning of the 3d of April, and the Federal army, leaving a small force to occupy Petersburg, set off in pursuit, following the line of the Southside railroad.

On the morning of the 3d the withdrawal of the Confederates from the lines of Richmond was discovered by General Weitzel, commanding the Federal forces on the north side of the James. MAJOR-GENERAL E. O. ORD. He at once advanced and occupied the city of Richmond, a large part of which was in flames as he entered it, having been set on fire by the Confederates upon their evacuation of it. Thus fell the Confederate capital after four long years of bloody war for its possession.

Upon reaching Amelia Court-house, General Lee found that the supplies he had ordered to be sent there from Danville were not to be had. The trains sent from Danville by his instructions had been ordered to Richmond to remove the property of the Confederate government, and had not been allowed to unload their stores at Amelia Court-house. This was a terrible blow to Lee, who was now unable to furnish food to his troops, who had eaten nothing since the commencement of the retreat. Parties were sent into the surrounding country to obtain supplies, and this consumed the whole of the 4th and 5th of April, which Lee had hoped to spend in pushing on beyond his pursuers. The delay enabled Sheridan, with eighteen thousand mounted men, to seize the Confederate

line of retreat at Jetersville. This movement put an end to Lee's hope of reaching Danville and joining Johnston. A battle was impossible, for Sheridan had a force nearly equal to his own, and Grant was hurrying on with the rest of the Federal army. General Lee therefore turned off and retreated towards Farmville, hoping to be able to reach Lynchburg, but Sheridan, after passing Farmville, pushed forward again, and by a forced march reached Appomattox Station, on the Southside railroad, on the night of the 8th, and planted his force squarely across the Confederate line of retreat. The next morning Lee, when near Appomattox Court-house, discovered this obstacle in his way, and about the same time Sheridan was joined by the army of the James, under General Ord, while the army of the Potomac, under General Meade, was closing in fast upon Lee's rear. General Lee had now but eight thousand men with arms in their hands. The bulk of his forces, being too much broken down by fatigue and hunger to keep their places in the ranks, accompanied the regiments in a disorganized mass. As soon as he discovered Sheridan in his front, Lee attempted to cut his way through his lines, but failing in this effort, and being convinced that further resistance would merely be a useless sacrifice of his men, he asked for a suspension of hostilities, and went to meet General Grant.

The two commanders met at a house near Appomattox Court-house, and after a brief interview arranged the terms of the surrender. General Grant treated the beaten army with great liberality. The hungry Confederates were fed by the victors, and after laying down their arms were permitted to return to their homes. In order that the men might betake themselves as soon as possible to the cultivation of the soil, and so avoid the suffering which the failure of the harvest would entail upon the south, General Grant released all captured horses which were identified as the property of the soldiers surrendering them. The terms of the surrender were arranged on the 9th of April. On the 12th the army of northern Virginia formed in divisions for the last time, and marching to a designated spot near Appomattox Court-house, laid down its arms, and disbanded. About seventy-five hundred men with arms, and about eighteen thousand unarmed stragglers, took part in the surrender. The Federal troops treated their vanquished opponents with true soldierly kindness, and carefully refrained from everything which might seem to insult the valor that had won their earnest admiration.

The news of the capture of Richmond and Petersburg and the surrender of Lee's army was received in the north with the greatest rejoicing. Bells were rung, cannon fired, and illuminations flashed from every town and village, for it was understood that these great successes were decisive of the war.

SURRENDER OF GENERAL LEE.

In the midst of these rejoicings occurred a terrible tragedy, which plunged the country into mourning. President Lincoln, whose re-election we have related, entered upon his second term on the 4th of March, 1865, amid the congratulations of the country. On the evening of the 14th of April he attended a performance at Ford's theatre, in the city of Washington. During the midst of the performance the report of a pistol rang through the house, and the next moment a man leaped from the president's box upon the stage, and waving a pistol over his head, shouted *" Sic semper tyrannis "* (Thus always with tyrants), and disappeared behind the scenes. The cry was raised that the president had been killed, and in the commotion which ensued the assassin escaped. The murderer had entered the lobby of the theatre, and had fired from the door of the private box upon the unsuspicious president, who was sitting with his back to him. Mr. Lincoln fell heavily forward and never spoke again. He was conveyed to a house on the opposite side of the street, and the highest skill was exerted to save him; but all in vain. He died on the morning of the 15th, surrounded by his family and the leading men of the nation. Appropriate funeral services were held on the 19th, and the body of the martyred president was conveyed through the principal cities of the north and west to Springfield, Illinois, where it was buried. Along the entire route it was received with the evidences of the nation's grief. Cities were draped in mourning, and dense crowds poured out to greet the funeral cortege and testify their love and sorrow for the dead man. Even in the south, which had made the election of Abraham Lincoln the occasion of the dissolution of the Union, the unaffected and manly virtues of this simply great man had conquered the people, who had come to regard him as their best and truest friend. His death was sincerely lamented there, and in the lamentation of the south Abraham Lincoln had his proudest triumph. His death was a crushing misfortune to the whole country. He was the only man capable of carrying out a policy of generous conciliation towards the south, and he had resolved upon such a course. He was sincerely desirous to heal the wounds of the war as soon as possible, and was strong enough to put down all opposition to his policy. His untimely death, as well as the manner of it, threw back the settlement of our national troubles fully five years.

As he leaped from the president's box to the stage the assassin's foot caught in an American flag with which the box was draped, and he fell heavily, breaking his leg. He managed to escape, however. It was immediately ascertained that the assassin was John Wilkes Booth, a younger son of the famous actor Junius Brutus Booth. Almost at the same time

MONUMENT TO ABRAHAM LINCOLN IN FAIRMOUNT PARK, PHILADELPHIA.

that the president was shot, another assassin, one Payne *alias* Powell, entered the residence of Secretary Seward. Proceeding to the chamber where the secretary was confined to a sick-bed, he attacked the two attendants of the invalid, and his son, Frederick W. Seward, and injured them severely, and then attempted to cut Mr. Seward's throat. He succeeded in gashing the face of his intended victim, but fled before further harm could be done.

Booth, who was most probably insane, had drawn quite a number of persons into a conspiracy, which had for its object the murder of the president and vice-president, Secretaries Seward and Stanton, and Chief Justice Chase. The plot failed through unexpected movements of some of the intended victims and the cowardice of some of the conspirators. Booth and a young man named Harold fled into lower Maryland, from which they crossed the Potomac into Virginia. They were pursued by the government detectives and a squadron of cavalry, and were tracked to a barn in Caroline county, Virginia, between Bowling Green and Port Royal. Here they were surrounded on the 26th of April. Harold surrendered himself, but Booth, refusing to yield, was shot by Sergeant Boston Corbett, and died a few hours later, after suffering intensely. His accomplices were arrested, and were brought to trial before a military commission at Washington. Payne or Powell, Atzerot, Harold, and Mrs. Surratt were condemned to death, and were hanged on the 7th of July, 1865, for complicity in the plot. Dr. Mudd, O'Laughlin and Arnold were imprisoned in the Dry Tortugas for life, and Spangler for six years. What Booth expected to accomplish by his horrible deed yet remains a mystery. It is now generally believed that he was insane ; rendered so perhaps by his dissipated habits—and in this state of mind had conceived the idea that Mr. Lincoln was a tyrant, and as such ought to be put to death. He had no accomplices in the south, and his bloody deed was regarded with horror by the southern people. We must now return to Sherman's army, which we left resting at Goldsboro'. Johnston's army was in the vicinity of Raleigh, and after the fall of Richmond was joined by Mr. Davis and the various officers of the Confederate government. On the 10th of April Sherman advanced from Goldsboro' towards Johnston's position, and steadily pressed the Confederate army back. On the 13th Sherman entered Raleigh. Being convinced that further resistance was hopeless, and having learned of the surrender of General Lee's army, General Johnston now opened negotiations with General Sherman for the surrender of his army to the Federal commander. The result of these negotiations was an agreement signed by the two commanders on the 18th of April. As this agreement provided for the restoration of the States of the Confederacy to their lost places in the Union, it was disapproved by the Federal government, and Sherman was ordered to resume hostilities. General Johnston was at once notified by General Sherman of this order, and on the 26th of April entered into an agreement with him by which he surrendered to General Sherman all the Confederate forces under his command, on terms similar to those granted to General Lee by General Grant.

HON. W. H. SEWARD.

LIEUT.-GEN. E. KIRBY SMITH.

INTERVIEW BETWEEN GENERALS SHERMAN AND JOHNSTON.

The example of Generals Lee and Johnston was followed by the other Confederate commanders throughout the south. The last to surrender was General E. Kirby Smith, in Texas, on the 26th of May. On the 29th of May President Johnson issued a proclamation announcing the close of the war, and offering amnesty to all who had participated in it on the Confederate side, with the exception of fourteen specified classes.

JUDAH P. BENJAMIN.

Upon the surrender of Johnston's army, Mr. Davis and the members of his former cabinet endeavored to make their way to the coast of Florida, from which they hoped to be able to reach the West Indies. Some of them succeeded in doing so, but Mr. Davis was captured at Irwinsville, Georgia, on the 10th of May, and was sent as a prisoner to Fortress Monroe, where he was held in confinement until May, 1867.

The civil war was over. It had cost the country one million of men in the killed and crippled for life of the two armies. In money the north and the south had expended probably the enormous sum of $5,000,000,-000. The exact amount will never be known, as the Confederate debt perished with the government which created it.

in this region, and the feeling between them and the patriots was one of the bitterest hostility, and often manifested itself in bloody and relentless conflicts. Seven hundred Tories under Colonel Boyd set out in February, 1779, to join Colonel Campbell at Augusta. On the 14th they were attacked at Kettle creek, by a force of patriots under Colonel Pickens, and were defeated with heavy loss. Pickens hung five of his prisoners as traitors.

General Lincoln now sent General Ashe with two thousand men to drive the British out of Augusta. Upon hearing of his approach Colonel Campbell evacuated Augusta and fell back to Brier creek, a small stream about halfway to Savannah. Ashe followed him, but without observing proper caution, and on the 3d of March was surprised and routed by Campbell, with the loss of nearly his entire force. This defeat encouraged General Prevost to attempt the capture of Charleston. He marched rapidly across the country to Charleston, and demanded its surrender. Lincoln, who had been reinforced, no sooner heard of this movement than he hastened by forced marches to the relief of Charleston, and compelled Prevost to retire to St. John's island, opposite the mainland. The British threw up a redoubt at Stone ferry to protect the crossing to this island. It was attacked on the 20th of June by the forces of General Lincoln, who were repulsed with heavy loss. A little later Prevost withdrew to Savannah. The intense heat of the weather suspended military operations in the south during the remainder of the summer.

In September, 1779, the French fleet under Count D'Estaing arrived off the coast of Georgia from the West Indies, and the admiral agreed to join Lincoln in an effort to recapture Savannah. The American army

GENERAL BENJAMIN LINCOLN.

near the centre of his line. The winter passed away without any event of importance. The British held New York and Newport with too strong a force to make an attack upon either post successful, and the withdrawal of the French fleet to the West Indies left Washington without any means of encountering the naval force of the enemy.

The season was not without its trials, however. Washington wrote at the beginning of the year 1779, " Our affairs are in a more distressed, ruinous, and deplorable condition than they have been since the commencement of the war." The currency of the country grew more worthless every day. During the year 1779 the enormous sum of one hunrded and thirty-one million of dollars was issued in continental bills. The magnitude of the volume of the currency only served to depreciate it more and more, and though supplies and articles of trade were plentiful, their owners refused to accept the depreciated bills of Congress, and would sell for gold and silver only. "A wagon-load of money," Washington wrote to the president of Congress, " will not purchase a wagon-load of provisions." During the year the currency depreciated from $8 for one dollar to $41.50 for one dollar. Congress had so little specie that everything must have gone to ruin but for the exertions of Robert Morris, a member of Congress from Pennsylvania, and a leading merchant of Philadelphia, who borrowed large sums of coin on his own credit, and loaned them to the government. This he continued to do throughout the war.

Congress had long before this been deprived of many of its ablest members, who had resigned their seats in order to accept appointments in their own States, or to enter the army. Their places were filled with weaker men, and many dissensions mark the deliberations of the Congress of this period. Many members of Congress and a large part of the people seemed to regard the alliance with France as decisive of the war, and were disposed to relax their efforts. During the winter it was proposed to join the French in an expedition for the recovery of Canada for France, and the scheme found favor with a majority of the delegates in Congress. Washington opposed it with firmness. He pointed out to Congress the difficulties of the undertaking, and declared his conviction that it was not to the interest of the United States that a power different in race, language and religion from the people of this republic should have a footing upon this continent. In addition to this he did not desire the people of the United States to increase their obligations to a foreign, even though a friendly, power.

The American forces in the Southern States were commanded by General Benjamin Lincoln. The Tories were very numerous and very active

BIRD'S-EYE VIEW OF NEW YORK CITY, SHOWING THE BRIDGE CONNECTING IT WITH BROOKLYN.

THE UNITED STATES TREASURY, WASHINGTON CITY.

www.ingramcontent.com/pod-product-compliance
Lightning Source LLC
Chambersburg PA
CBHW021412090426
42742CB00009B/1111